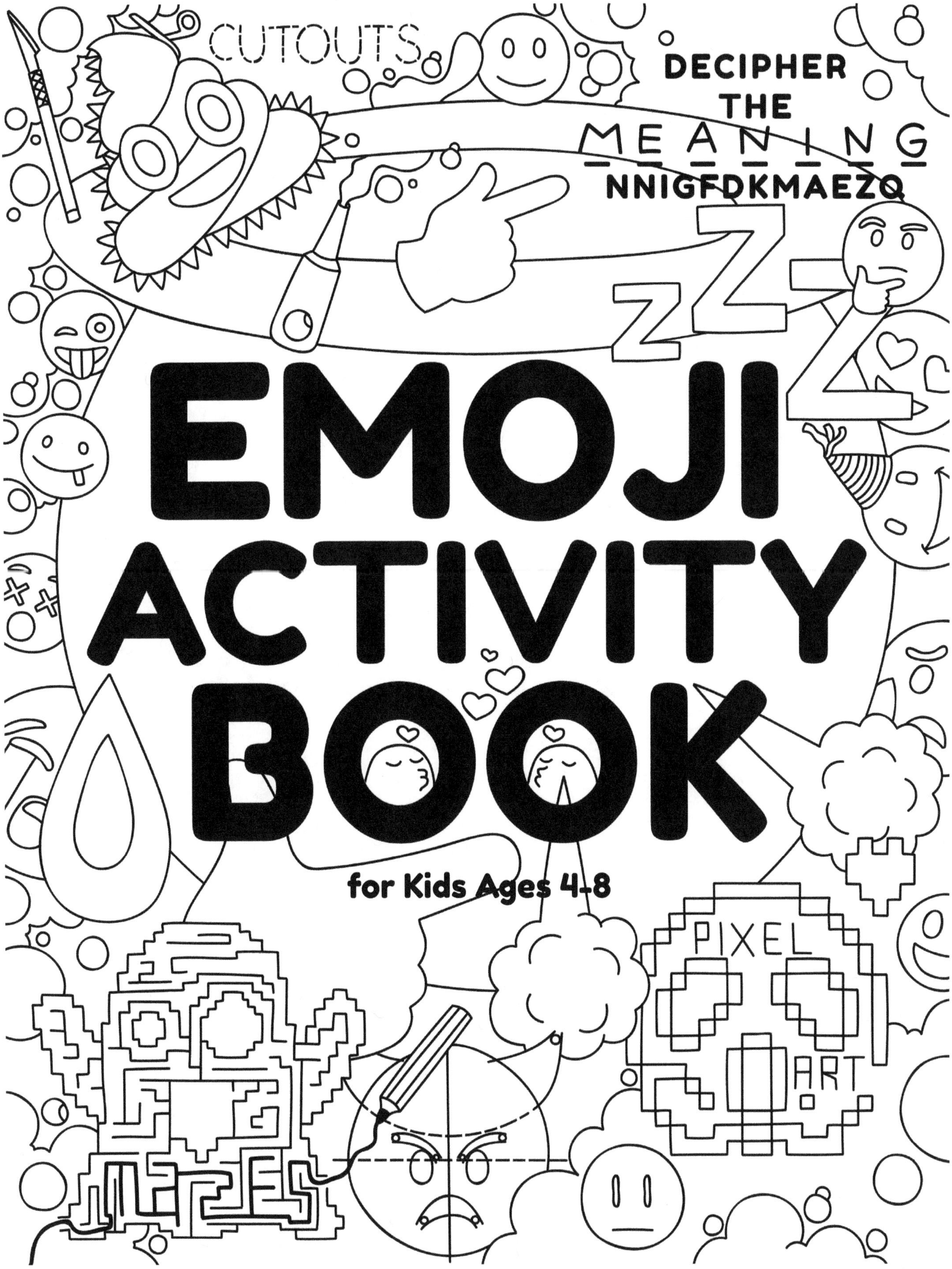
CUTOUTS
DECIPHER
THE
MEANING
NNIGFDKMAEZQ
EMOJI
ACTIVITY
BOOK
for Kids Ages 4-8
PIXEL
ART
MAZES

COLORING PAGES

Color these pages!

1

2

3

4

5

6

7

COLORING PAGES WITH COLOR GUIDES

Color the image below according to the given color guide.

1

1. Yellow	3. Brown	5. Red	7. Pink	9. Violet
2. Olive green	4. Blue	6. Green	8. Orange	

2

1. Red
2. Orange
3. Yellow
4. Green
5. Blue
6. Indigo
7. Violet
8. Brown

3

1. Yellow
2. Orange
3. Red
4. Pink
5. Blue
6. Brown
7. Green

4

1. Yellow
2. Orange
3. Pink
4. Brown
5. Blue
6. Indigo
7. Green
8. Red

5

1. Yellow
2. Brown
3. Green
4. Indigo
5. Red
6. Blue

DOT-TO-DOT

Beginning with number 1, connect the dots in numerical order to reveal the fun emojis. You can color and decorate your work if you want to.

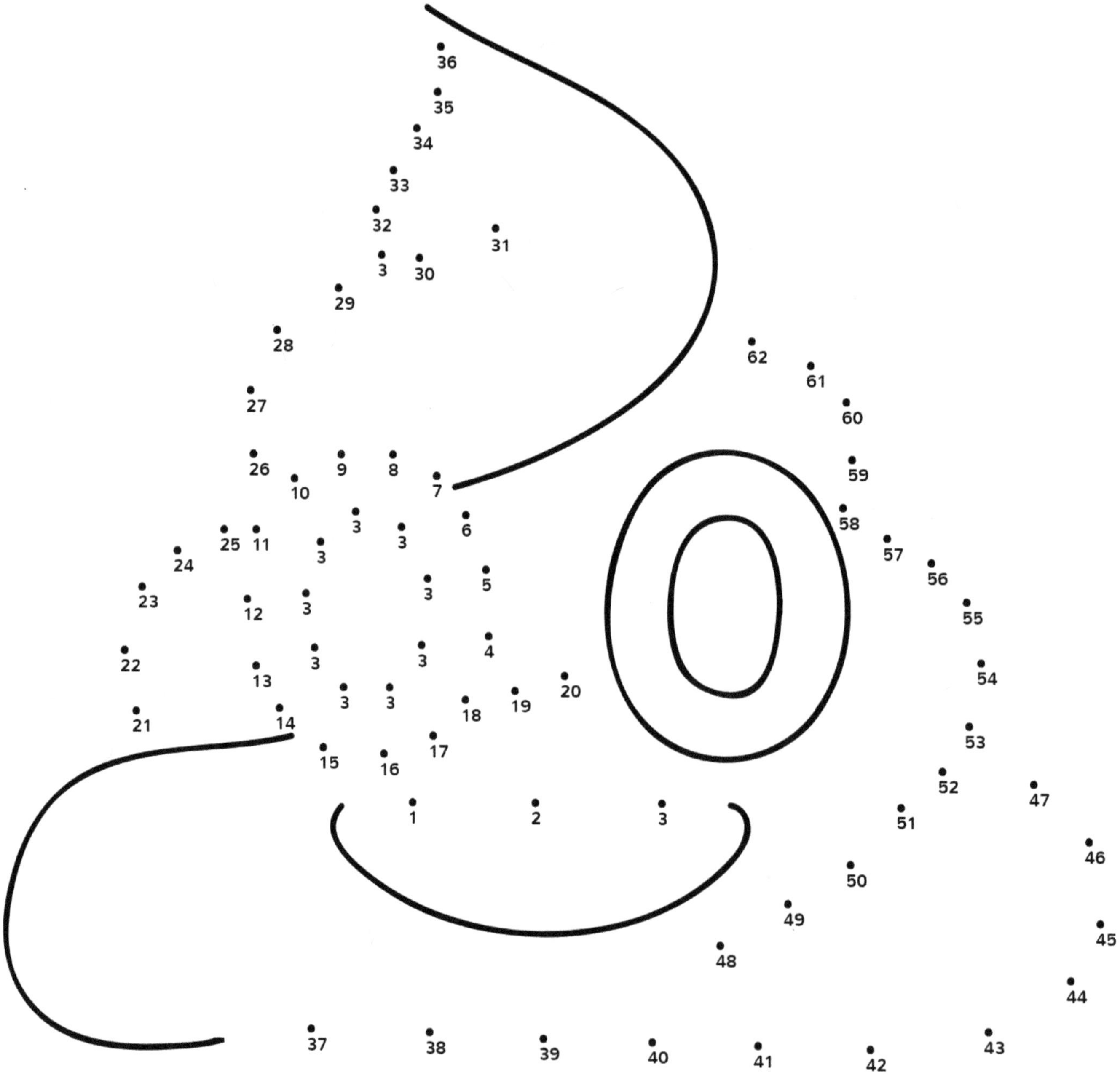

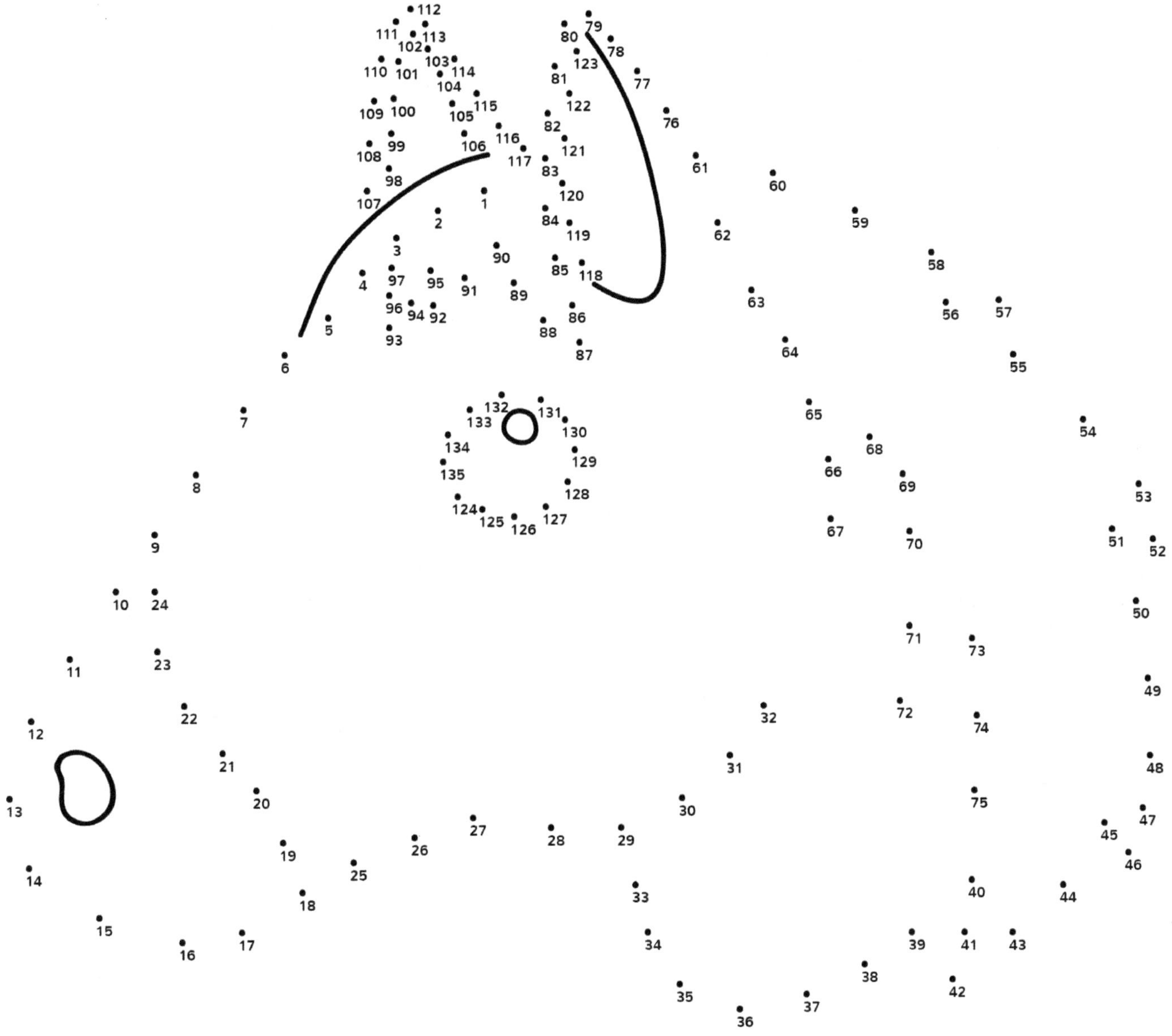

1
2
3
4
5
6
7
8
9
10
11
12
13
14
15
16
17
18
19
20
21
22
23
24
25
26
27
28
29
30
31
32
33
34
35
36
37
38
39
40
41
42
43
44
45
46
47
48
49
50
51
52
53
54
55
56
57
58
59
60
61
62
63
64
65
66
67
68
69
70
71
72
73
74
75
76
77
78
79
80
81
82
83
84
85
86
87
88
89
90
91
92
93
94
95
96
97
98
99
100
101
102
103
104
105
106
107
108
109
110
111
112
113
114
115
116
117
118
119
120
121
122
123
124
125
126
127
128
129
130
131
132
133
134
135

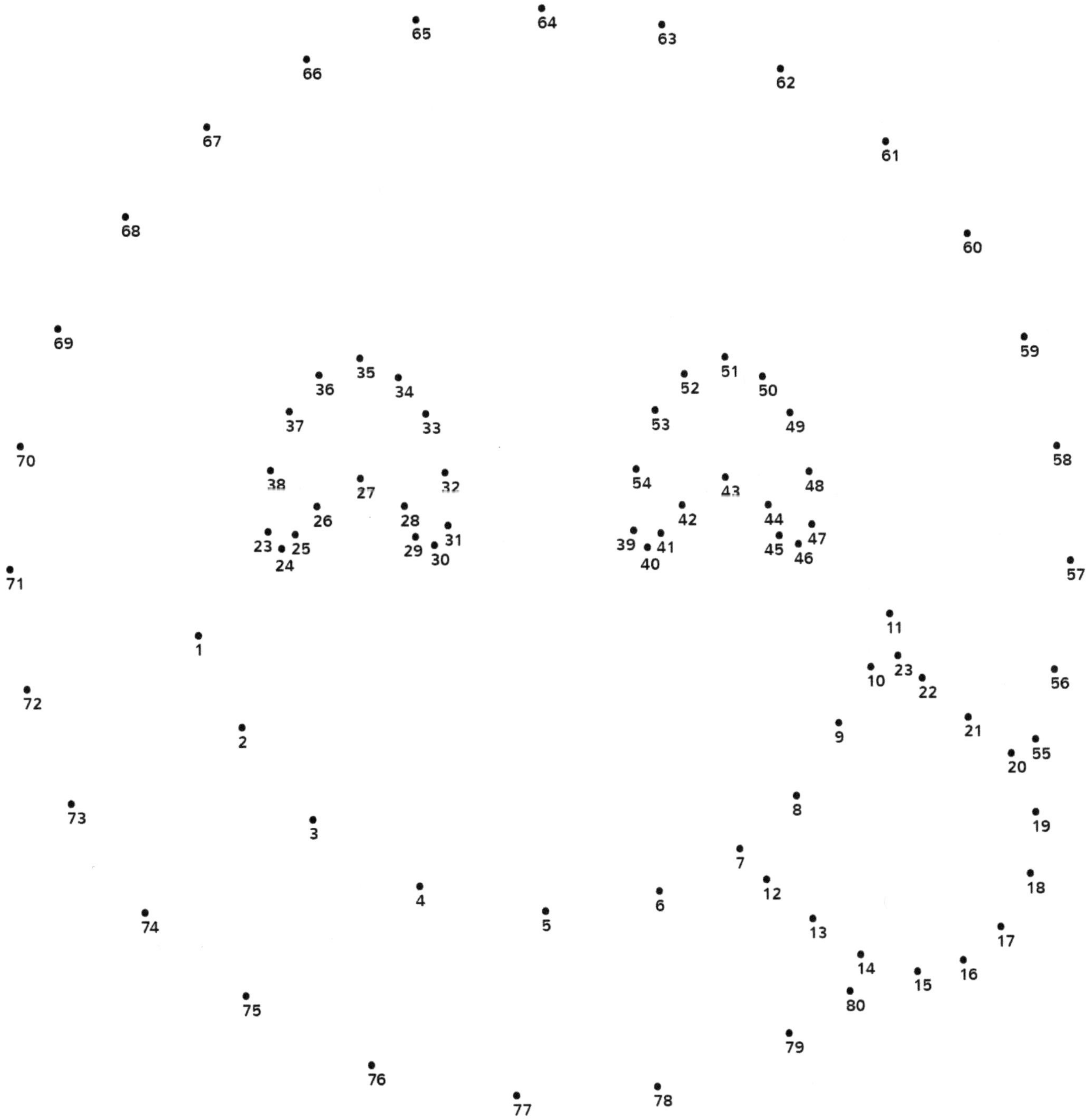
1
2
3
4
5
6
7
8
9
10
11
12
13
14
15
16
17
18
19
20
21
22
23
23
24
25
26
27
28
29
30
31
32
33
34
35
36
37
38
39
40
41
42
43
44
45
46
47
48
49
50
51
52
53
54
55
56
57
58
59
60
61
62
63
64
65
66
67
68
69
70
71
72
73
74
75
76
77
78
79
80

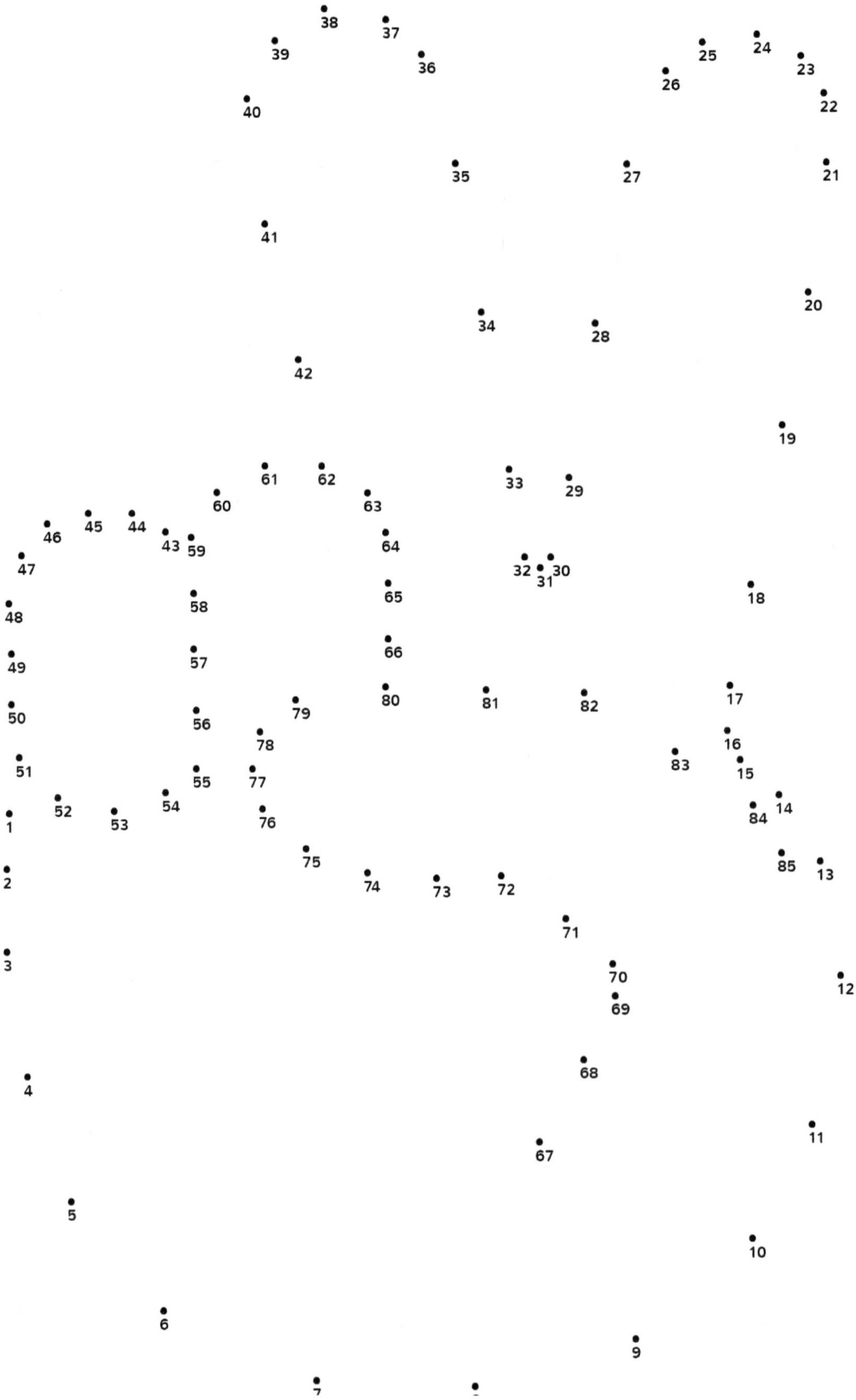
1
2
3
4
5
6
7
9
10
11
12
13
14
15
16
17
18
19
20
21
22
23
24
25
26
27
28
29
30
31
32
33
34
35
36
37
38
39
40
41
42
43
44
45
46
47
48
49
50
51
52
53
54
55
56
57
58
59
60
61
62
63
64
65
66
67
68
69
70
71
72
73
74
75
76
77
78
79
80
81
82
83
84
85

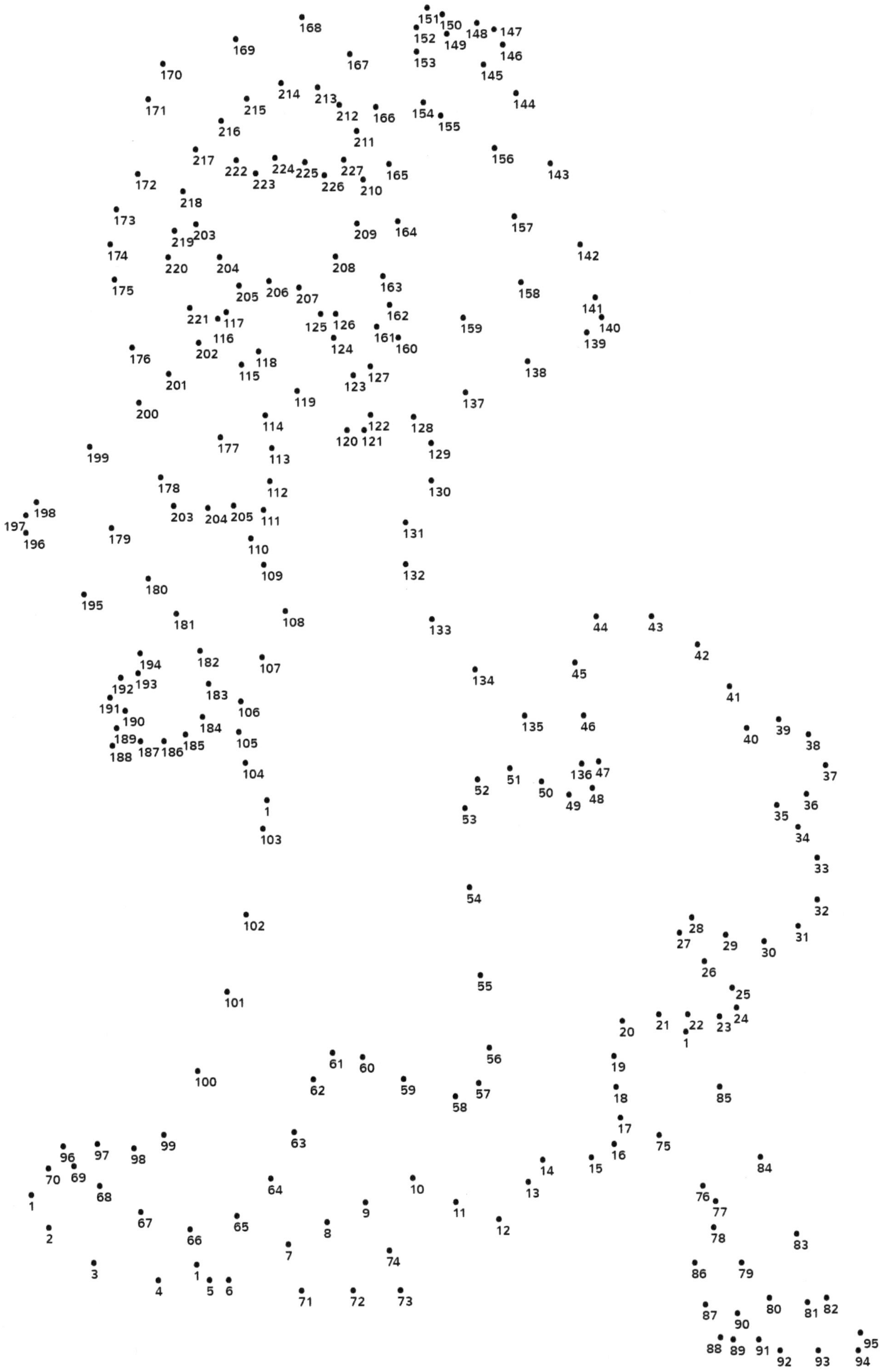

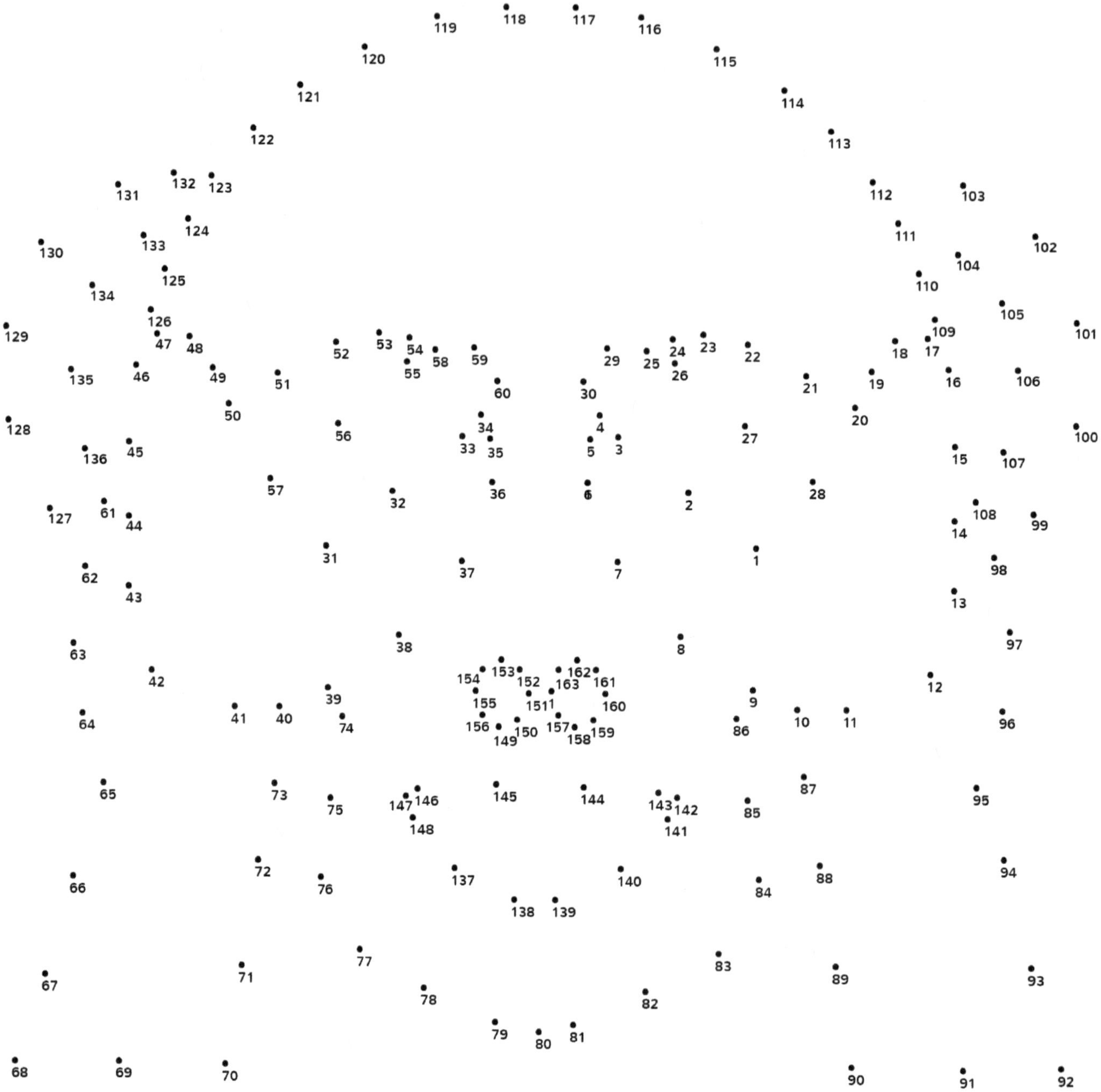

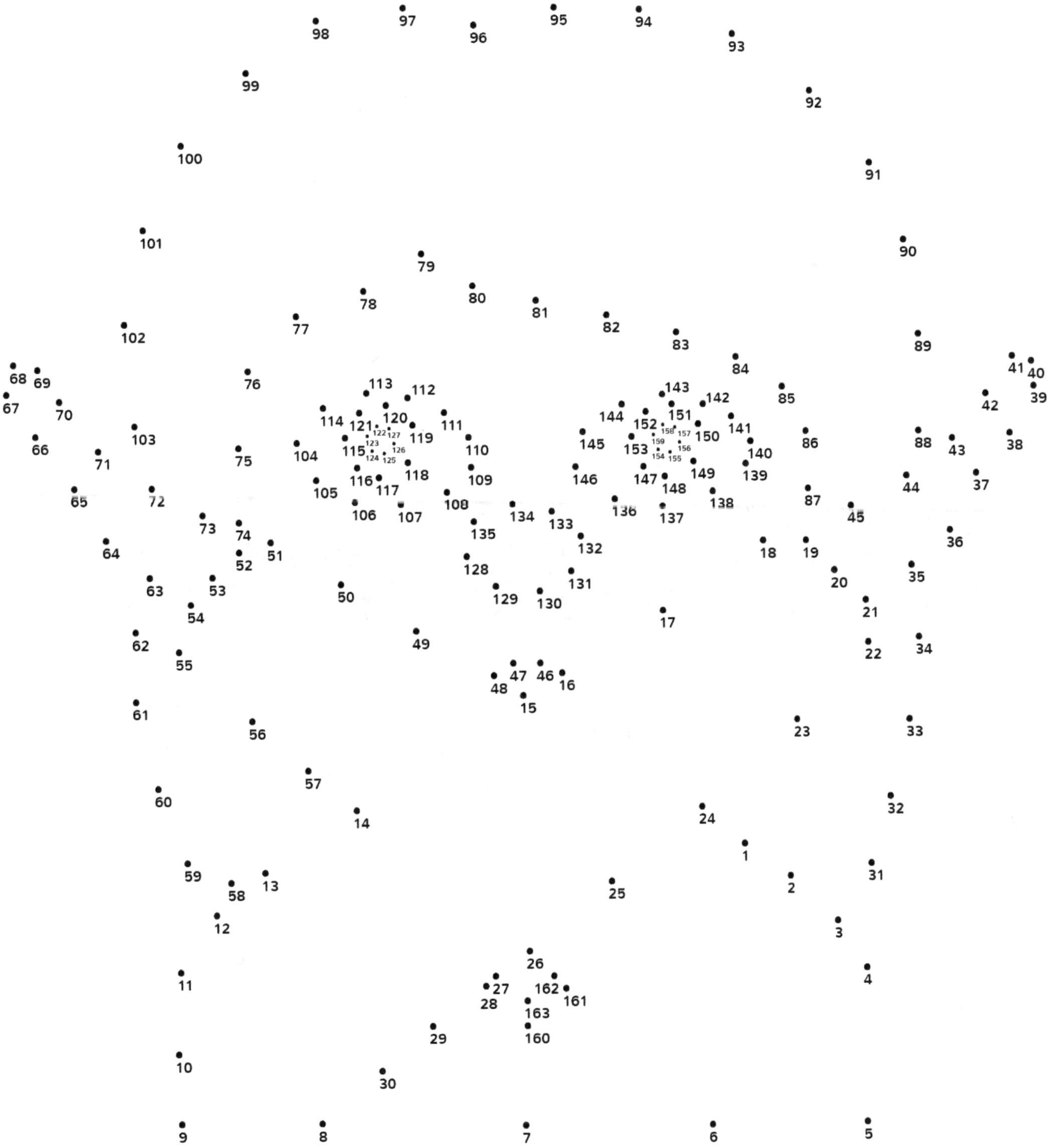

PIXEL MATH

Solve the math problems and refer to the color guide with your answer. Then color the squares according to the color guide.

Unicorn

2 x6	11 x1	3 x6	2 x5	9 x1	3 x2	11 x1	2 x5	9 x1	3 x2	9 x1	3 x2	2 x6	11 x1	2 x5	9 x1	3 x2	9 x1	3 x2	2 x6	11 x1	2 x5	9 x1	3 x2
4 x4	8 x5	4 x4	20 x1	4 x4	3 x5	4 x4	20 x1	4 x4	3 x5	4 x4	3 x5	9 x1	4 x4	20 x1	4 x4	3 x5	4 x4	3 x5	9 x1	4 x4	20 x1	4 x4	3 x5
11 x1	3 x6	11 x3	5 x8	9 x1	3 x2	9 x1	3 x2	2 x6	11 x1	2 x6	11 x1	2 x5	9 x1	3 x2	2 x6	11 x1	2 x6	11 x1	2 x5	9 x1	3 x2	2 x6	11 x1
20 x1	4 x4	6 x6	9 x1	4 x9	3 x5	4 x4	3 x5	9 x1	4 x4	9 x1	4 x4	20 x1	4 x4	3 x5	9 x1	4 x4	9 x1	4 x4	20 x1	4 x4	3 x5	9 x1	4 x4
2 x5	9 x1	3 x2	7 x3	4 x4	11 x3	9 x1	3 x2	4 x4	11 x1	2 x6	11 x1	2 x5	9 x1	3 x2	4 x4	11 x1	2 x6	11 x1	2 x5	9 x1	3 x2	4 x4	11 x1
20 x1	4 x4	3 x5	8 x5	11 x1	9 x1	5 x8	9 x1	3 x2	2 x6	11 x1	3 x6	8 x5	9 x1	3 x2	11 x3	20 x1	4 x4	3 x5	9 x1	4 x4	20 x1	4 x4	3 x5
3 x2	9 x1	3 x2	20 x1	5 x8	20 x1	4 x4	4 x9	2 x5	9 x1	4 x4	4 x9	25 x5	11 x3	7 x3	2 x6	5 x8	9 x1	3 x2	2 x6	11 x1	2 x5	9 x1	3 x2
11 x1	4 x4	3 x5	9 x1	3 x2	4 x9	4 x4	3 x5	6 x6	4 x4	11 x1	11 x3	16 x10	15 x9	8 x5	32 x5	4 x4	4 x9	11 x1	2 x5	9 x1	3 x2	2 x6	11 x1
4 x4	2 x6	11 x1	4 x4	3 x5	20 x1	6 x6	9 x1	3 x2	7 x3	8 x8	7 x8	22 x2	7 x7	15 x5	16 x10	11 x1	3 x6	15 x5	20 x1	4 x4	3 x5	9 x1	4 x4
11 x1	9 x1	4 x4	2 x6	11 x1	3 x2	9 x1	7 x3	11 x1	11 x10	7 x9	16 x3	20 x4	11 x4	20 x4	9 x1	3 x2	16 x5	22 x2	20 x4	9 x1	3 x2	2 x6	11 x1
9 x1	4 x4	11 x1	9 x1	4 x4	3 x5	4 x4	11 x1	5 x8	9 x1	4 x4	33 x2	9 x1	15 x5	20 x1	4 x4	3 x5	8 x8	6 x8	11 x4	7 x9	11 x1	2 x5	9 x1
3 x5	4 x4	3 x5	4 x4	11 x1	3 x2	2 x6	7 x3	2 x5	9 x1	3 x2	11 x1	2 x5	9 x1	3 x2	2 x6	11 x1	7 x9	7 x8	22 x2	7 x7	15 x5	4 x4	3 x5
11 x1	9 x1	3 x2	9 x1	3 x2	20 x1	9 x3	9 x1	20 x1	4 x4	3 x5	4 x4	20 x1	4 x4	3 x5	9 x1	4 x4	15 x5	16 x3	6 x8	11 x4	6 x8	20 x4	11 x1
4 x4	2 x6	11 x1	4 x4	3 x5	8 x5	11 x1	11 x1	2 x5	17 x10	19 x10	11 x1	2 x5	9 x1	3 x2	4 x4	11 x1	20 x4	11 x4	16 x3	7 x8	22 x2	11 x3	4 x4
11 x1	9 x1	4 x4	11 x1	11 x3	3 x5	9 x1	3 x2	2 x6	21 x9	11 x20	9 x1	3 x2	2 x5	9 x1	3 x2	33 x2	20 x1	15 x5	7 x8	22 x2	11 x4	6 x6	11 x1
3 x5	2 x6	11 x1	6 x6	15 x9	11 x1	4 x4	3 x5	9 x1	4 x4	20 x1	4 x4	3 x5	11 x1	2 x5	9 x1	3 x2	9 x1	4 x4	7 x9	20 x4	16 x3	7 x3	3 x5
3 x2	2 x5	7 x3	12 x11	13 x10	4 x4	2 x6	11 x1	2 x5	9 x1	3 x2	2 x6	11 x1	4 x4	20 x1	4 x4	3 x5	2 x5	11 x1	15 x5	3 x5	16 x5	8 x5	3 x2
11 x1	5 x8	12 x11	4 x9	25 x5	12 x11	9 x1	4 x4	20 x1	4 x4	3 x5	9 x1	4 x4	20 x1	3 x2	2 x6	11 x1	9 x1	3 x2	2 x6	11 x1	11 x3	5 x8	11 x1
4 x4	11 x3	15 x9	25 x5	12 x11	15 x9	2 x6	11 x1	2 x5	9 x1	3 x2	4 x4	11 x1	22 x4	11 x9	15 x6	11 x10	4 x4	3 x5	9 x1	4 x4	100 x1	6 x6	4 x4
11 x1	6 x6	13 x10	15 x9	25 x5	32 x5	13 x10	50 x2	22 x4	11 x9	15 x6	9 x9	100 x1	11 x10	60 x2	26 x4	3 x5	2 x6	11 x1	2 x5	11 x1	9 x9	4 x9	11 x1
9 x1	4 x9	25 x5	12 x11	16 x10	25 x5	15 x9	7 x3	5 x8	11 x3	6 x6	7 x3	5 x8	9 x3	12 x9	2 x6	11 x1	9 x1	4 x4	20 x1	15 x6	22 x4	11 x3	9 x1
3 x5	20 x1	8 x5	11 x3	7 x3	6 x6	9 x3	9 x1	3 x2	2 x6	11 x1	2 x5	9 x1	3 x2	5 x8	9 x1	4 x4	2 x6	11 x1	2 x5	22 x4	9 x9	5 x8	3 x5
9 x1	3 x2	2 x6	11 x1	2 x5	9 x1	3 x2	4 x4	3 x5	9 x1	4 x4	20 x1	4 x4	3 x5	6 x6	11 x1	2 x5	9 x1	3 x2	9 x9	100 x1	22 x4	6 x6	11 x1
4 x4	3 x5	9 x1	4 x4	20 x1	4 x4	3 x5	2 x6	11 x1	2 x5	9 x1	3 x2	2 x6	11 x1	4 x9	9 x1	3 x2	9 x9	100 x1	22 x4	11 x9	15 x6	4 x9	4 x4
2 x6	11 x1	2 x5	9 x1	3 x2	2 x6	11 x1	9 x1	4 x4	20 x1	4 x4	3 x5	9 x1	4 x4	11 x3	50 x2	22 x4	11 x9	15 x6	9 x9	100 x1	22 x4	11 x3	11 x1
9 x1	4 x4	20 x1	4 x4	3 x5	9 x1	4 x4	2 x6	11 x1	2 x5	9 x1	3 x2	4 x4	11 x1	2 x6	5 x8	11 x3	7 x3	6 x6	9 x3	7 x3	5 x8	2 x6	3 x5
2 x6	11 x1	2 x5	9 x1	3 x2	4 x4	11 x1	4 x4	3 x5	9 x1	4 x4	20 x1	4 x4	3 x5	4 x4	2 x6	11 x1	2 x5	9 x1	3 x2	4 x4	11 x1	9 x1	3 x2

1-20 - Blank
21-40 - Brown
41-60 - Pink
61-80 - Purple
81-100 - Grey
101-120 - Dark grey
121-140 - Light pink
141-160 - Pale pink
161-180 - Indigo
181-200 - Blue
201-220 - Navy

Woman Tipping Hand Emoji

6x3	8x2	6x3	8x2	4x4	3x5	1x1	8x2	6x3	3x5	1x1	5x4	8x2	4x4	3x5	1x1	5x4	4x4	3x5	20x1	4x4	20x1	6x3	4x4	20x1	6x3	8x2
4x4	3x5	1x1	4x4	3x5	8x2	40x1	2x16	11x2	15x2	11x2	15x2	2x16	11x2	15x2	11x2	6x3	1x1	8x2	6x3	3x5	1x1	5x4	8x2	4x4	3x5	1x1
1x1	5x4	4x4	1x1	8x2	40x1	12x3	11x2	40x1	11x2	40x1	11x2	11x2	40x1	11x2	2x16	40x1	6x3	3x5	1x1	5x4	8x2	4x4	3x5	1x1	5x4	4x4
8x2	4x4	3x5	15x2	11x2	2x16	40x1	2x16	11x2	15x2	11x2	15x2	2x16	11x2	15x2	11x2	2x16	40x1	1x1	8x2	6x3	3x5	1x1	5x4	8x2	4x4	3x5
3x5	1x1	40x1	11x2	2x16	11x2	12x3	11x2	40x1	11x2	40x1	11x2	11x2	40x1	11x2	2x16	11x2	12x3	11x2	6x3	3x5	1x1	5x4	8x2	4x4	3x5	1x1
5x4	4x4	11x2	2x16	11x2	2x16	40x1	2x16	11x2	2x16	11x2	40x1	2x16	11x2	2x16	11x2	2x16	40x1	2x16	1x1	5x4	8x2	4x4	3x5	1x1	5x4	4x4
8x2	11x2	2x16	15x2	2x16	11x2	12x3	11x2	2x16	15x2	2x16	15x2	11x2	2x16	15x2	2x16	11x2	12x3	11x2	2x16	6x3	3x5	1x1	5x4	8x2	4x4	3x5
1x1	2x16	11x2	12x3	11x2	2x16	40x1	12x3	25x2	2x16	11x2	12x3	2x16	11x2	12x3	11x2	2x16	40x1	2x16	11x2	4x4	20x1	6x3	4x4	20x1	6x3	8x2
4x4	11x2	2x16	40x1	2x16	11x2	12x3	25x2	6x9	10x6	2x16	40x1	11x2	2x16	40x1	2x16	11x2	12x3	11x2	2x16	3x5	1x1	5x4	8x2	4x4	3x5	1x1
3x5	2x16	15x2	11x2	25x2	10x6	25x2	10x6	10x6	25x2	10x6	25x2	10x6	25x2	10x6	11x2	2x16	40x1	2x16	15x2	5x4	8x2	4x4	3x5	1x1	5x4	4x4
1x1	15x2	11x2	25x2	19x3	6x9	10x6	6x9	10x6	19x3	25x2	19x3	6x9	10x6	6x9	10x6	6x9	11x2	15x2	11x2	6x3	3x5	1x1	5x4	8x2	4x4	3x5
4x4	12x3	2x16	10x6	19x3	3x5	1x1	3x5	6x9	10x6	6x9	10x6	19x3	3x5	1x1	3x5	25x2	6x9	12x3	2x16	3x5	1x1	5x4	8x2	4x4	3x5	1x1
3x5	40x1	15x2	6x9	6x3	5x4	15x2	5x4	8x2	6x9	10x6	6x9	6x3	5x4	2x16	5x4	8x2	10x6	40x1	15x2	5x4	8x2	4x4	3x5	1x1	5x4	4x4
8x2	11x2	12x3	10x6	19x3	6x3	3x5	6x3	6x9	10x6	6x9	10x6	19x3	6x3	3x5	6x3	6x9	25x2	11x2	12x3	6x3	3x5	1x1	5x4	8x2	4x4	3x5
1x1	2x16	40x1	10x6	25x2	10x6	25x2	25x2	10x6	25x2	10x6	25x2	6x9	10x6	25x2	10x6	25x2	10x6	2x16	40x1	3x5	1x1	5x4	8x2	4x4	3x5	1x1
4x4	11x2	11x2	6x9	10x6	6x9	10x6	19x3	6x9	10x6	6x9	10x6	19x3	6x9	10x6	6x9	10x6	6x9	11x2	11x2	6x9	10x6	25x2	10x6	25x2	10x6	8x2
3x5	2x16	2x16	10x6	6x9	10x6	6x9	25x2	10x6	6x9	10x6	6x9	25x2	10x6	6x9	10x6	6x9	2x16	12x3	25x2	10x6	25x2	10x6	1x1	5x4	8x2	1x1
1x1	15x2	11x2	2x16	10x6	6x9	10x6	55x2	20x6	6x9	10x6	25x2	30x4	22x5	10x6	6x9	10x6	11x2	15x2	10x6	6x9	10x6	4x4	3x5	1x1	5x4	4x4
4x4	12x3	2x16	12x3	11x2	10x6	6x9	25x2	30x4	22x5	55x2	20x6	120x1	10x6	6x9	10x6	15x2	40x1	2x16	9x8	9x7	9x8	1x1	5x4	8x2	4x4	3x5
3x5	2x16	11x2	15x2	2x16	12x3	10x6	19x3	10x6	30x4	120x1	55x2	25x2	19x3	6x9	12x3	2x16	12x3	11x2	40x2	31x2	40x2	5x4	8x2	4x4	3x5	1x1
1x1	12x3	15x2	2x16	11x2	15x2	2x16	25x2	25x2	19x3	25x2	19x3	6x9	25x2	11x2	2x16	11x2	15x2	2x16	9x7	9x8	9x7	4x4	3x5	1x1	5x4	4x4
8x2	1x1	12x3	11x2	2x16	40x1	11x2	12x3	10x6	25x2	10x6	25x2	25x2	15x2	2x16	12x3	15x2	2x16	11x2	31x2	40x2	31x2	1x1	5x4	8x2	4x4	3x5
1x1	4x4	40x1	2x16	11x2	12x3	9x7	15x6	6x9	10x6	6x9	10x6	19x3	10x9	9x8	15x5	2x16	11x2	15x2	15x5	9x7	15x5	6x3	4x4	20x1	6x3	8x2
4x4	8x2	4x4	3x5	40x2	9x7	40x2	25x4	10x6	6x9	10x6	6x9	25x2	45x2	31x2	9x7	31x2	9x7	11x2	9x7	31x2	9x7	5x4	8x2	4x4	3x5	1x1
3x5	1x1	8x2	9x8	15x5	9x8	15x5	9x8	9x9	6x9	10x6	6x9	10x9	9x8	15x5	9x8	15x5	9x8	8x2	9x8	15x5	9x8	4x4	3x5	1x1	5x4	4x4
1x1	3x5	9x7	40x2	9x7	40x2	9x7	40x2	9x7	25x4	45x2	25x4	9x7	40x2	9x7	40x2	9x7	40x2	5x4	40x2	9x7	40x2	1x1	5x4	8x2	4x4	3x5
4x4	1x1	9x8	9x7	9x8	9x7	9x8	9x7	9x8	9x7	9x8	9x7	9x8	9x7	9x8	9x7	9x8	9x7	4x4	9x7	9x8	9x7	5x4	8x2	4x4	3x5	1x1
3x5	4x4	40x2	15x5	40x2	15x5	40x2	15x5	40x2	15x5	40x2	15x5	40x2	15x5	40x2	15x5	40x2	15x5	3x5	15x5	40x2	15x5	4x4	3x5	1x1	5x4	4x4
8x2	1x1	9x7	9x8	9x7	9x8	9x7	9x8	9x7	9x8	9x7	9x8	9x7	9x8	9x7	9x8	9x7	9x8	40x2	9x8	9x7	9x8	1x1	5x4	8x2	4x4	3x5
6x3	8x2	3x2	1x11	5x4	8x2	3x2	6x3	8x2	3x2	1x11	5x4	8x2	3x2	8x2	3x2	1x11	5x4	6x3	8x2	3x2	1x11	5x4	8x2	1x11	5x4	6x3

1-20 - Blank
21-40 - Brown
41-60 - Yellow
61-80 - Pink
81-100 - Red
101-120 - Black

Ghost

5x4	1x1	4x4	3x5	20x1	1x1	4x4	1x1	4x4	3x5	20x1	5x4	1x1	4x4	3x5	20x1	1x1	4x4	20x1	1x1	4x4	1x1	4x4	3x5	20x1	5x4	1x1
6x3	8x2	3x2	1x11	5x4	8x2	3x2	8x2	3x2	1x11	5x4	6x3	8x2	3x2	1x11	5x4	8x2	3x2	5x4	8x2	3x2	8x2	3x2	1x11	5x4	6x3	8x2
5x4	1x1	4x4	3x5	20x1	1x1	4x4	1x1	4x4	3x5	20x1	5x4	1x1	4x4	3x5	20x1	1x1	4x4	20x1	1x1	4x4	1x1	4x4	3x5	20x1	5x4	1x1
8x2	3x2	5x4	8x2	3x2	8x2	3x2	1x11	5x4	6x3	8x2	2x16	11x2	15x2	2x16	12x3	8x2	3x2	5x4	8x2	3x2	8x2	3x2	1x11	5x4	6x3	8x2
5x4	1x1	4x4	3x5	20x1	1x1	4x4	1x1	4x4	12x3	11x2	19x3	6x9	25x2	10x6	6x9	2x16	11x2	4x4	1x1	5x4	1x1	4x4	3x5	20x1	1x1	4x4
6x3	8x2	3x2	1x11	5x4	8x2	3x2	8x2	15x2	6x9	25x2	6x9	25x2	10x6	6x9	10x6	19x3	6x9	40x1	8x2	6x3	8x2	3x2	1x11	5x4	8x2	3x2
5x4	1x1	4x4	3x5	20x1	1x1	4x4	40x1	6x9	10x6	19x3	10x6	19x3	6x9	10x6	6x9	25x2	10x6	6x9	2x16	5x4	1x1	4x4	3x5	20x1	1x1	4x4
8x2	3x2	5x4	8x2	3x2	8x2	3x2	11x2	25x2	6x9	25x2	6x9	25x2	10x6	6x9	10x6	19x3	6x9	10x6	11x2	8x2	3x2	5x4	8x2	3x2	8x2	3x2
3x5	20x1	2x16	20x1	8x2	3x2	15x2	10x6	19x3	25x2	6x9	25x2	6x9	10x6	19x3	9x7	9x8	10x6	25x2	6x9	15x2	8x2	1x1	4x4	2x16	1x1	3x5
3x2	12x3	10x6	11x2	1x1	4x4	12x3	6x9	25x2	6x9	10x6	6x9	10x6	6x9	40x2	9x8	40x2	9x8	6x9	10x6	12x3	1x1	5x4	11x2	6x9	12x3	3x2
4x4	40x1	6x9	10x6	15x2	5x4	40x1	25x2	6x9	40x2	9x8	10x6	6x9	31x2	9x7	40x2	9x7	40x2	9x7	6x9	40x1	8x2	15x2	6x9	10x6	40x1	4x4
5x4	11x2	10x6	6x9	25x2	2x16	11x2	6x9	10x6	9x7	40x2	25x2	19x3	15x5	31x2	9x7	31x2	9x7	9x8	19x3	11x2	2x16	25x2	10x6	25x2	11x2	5x4
8x2	3x2	15x2	10x6	6x9	25x2	2x16	25x2	10x6	6x9	25x2	10x6	6x9	10x6	15x5	40x2	15x5	40x2	19x3	6x9	2x16	19x3	6x9	25x2	15x2	3x5	8x2
3x5	20x1	12x3	6x9	25x2	10x6	11x2	10x6	6x9	10x6	19x3	6x9	10x6	6x9	25x2	10x6	6x9	19x3	6x9	25x2	11x2	6x9	25x2	10x6	12x3	3x2	3x5
8x2	3x2	5x4	11x2	19x3	6x9	2x16	25x2	10x6	40x2	6x9	10x6	6x9	10x6	19x3	6x9	10x6	15x5	10x6	19x3	2x16	10x6	19x3	11x2	8x2	3x2	5x4
5x4	1x1	4x4	2x16	25x2	10x6	15x2	19x3	25x2	19x3	9x7	9x9	25x4	45x2	25x4	10x9	31x2	10x6	6x9	25x2	15x2	6x9	25x2	2x16	5x4	1x1	4x4
6x3	8x2	3x2	20x1	40x1	6x9	12x3	25x2	10x6	25x2	25x2	15x6	45x2	28x4	9x9	45x2	10x6	6x9	25x2	6x9	12x3	19x3	40x1	8x2	6x3	8x2	3x2
3x2	1x11	5x4	6x3	8x2	15x2	6x9	10x6	6x9	10x6	19x3	25x4	22x5	55x2	20x6	25x4	6x9	10x6	6x9	10x6	19x3	40x1	3x2	1x11	5x4	6x3	8x2
4x4	3x5	20x1	5x4	1x1	12x3	10x6	6x9	10x6	6x9	25x2	9x9	30x4	120x1	55x2	9x9	10x6	6x9	10x6	6x9	25x2	11x2	4x4	3x5	20x1	5x4	1x1
3x2	1x11	5x4	6x3	8x2	40x1	25x2	19x3	25x2	19x3	6x9	55x2	14x8	110x1	28x4	30x4	25x2	19x3	25x2	19x3	6x9	2x16	3x2	1x11	5x4	6x3	8x2
4x4	3x5	20x1	1x1	4x4	11x2	10x6	25x2	10x6	25x2	25x2	25x2	30x4	120x1	55x2	19x3	10x6	25x2	10x6	6x9	25x2	11x2	4x4	3x5	20x1	1x1	4x4
8x2	3x2	5x4	5x4	11x2	19x3	6x9	10x6	6x9	10x6	19x3	10x6	6x9	25x2	6x9	25x2	6x9	10x6	6x9	10x6	19x3	10x6	15x2	5x4	8x2	3x2	5x4
5x4	1x1	4x4	20x1	2x16	25x2	10x6	6x9	10x6	6x9	25x2	6x9	19x3	10x6	19x3	10x6	25x2	6x9	10x6	6x9	25x2	6x9	12x3	20x1	5x4	1x1	4x4
6x3	8x2	3x2	40x1	6x9	10x6	6x9	2x16	11x2	2x16	6x9	10x6	6x9	25x2	6x9	6x9	10x6	15x2	11x2	25x2	6x9	10x6	6x9	2x16	6x3	8x2	3x2
3x2	1x11	11x2	2x16	2x16	6x9	15x2	2x16	3x2	1x11	15x2	2x16	25x2	6x9	19x3	11x2	2x16	3x2	1x11	15x2	2x16	6x9	25x2	15x2	11x2	6x3	8x2
20x1	5x4	1x1	2x16	11x2	15x2	4x4	1x1	4x4	3x5	20x1	5x4	2x16	11x2	15x2	4x4	1x1	4x4	3x5	20x1	5x4	11x2	2x16	12x3	20x1	5x4	1x1
6x3	8x2	3x2	1x11	5x4	8x2	3x2	8x2	3x2	1x11	5x4	6x3	8x2	3x2	1x11	5x4	8x2	3x2	5x4	8x2	3x2	8x2	3x2	1x11	5x4	6x3	8x2
5x4	1x1	4x4	3x5	20x1	1x1	4x4	1x1	4x4	3x5	20x1	5x4	1x1	4x4	3x5	20x1	1x1	4x4	20x1	1x1	4x4	1x1	4x4	3x5	20x1	5x4	1x1
6x3	8x2	3x2	1x11	5x4	8x2	3x2	8x2	3x2	1x11	5x4	6x3	8x2	3x2	1x11	5x4	8x2	3x2	5x4	8x2	3x2	8x2	3x2	1x11	5x4	6x3	8x2
5x4	1x1	4x4	3x5	20x1	1x1	4x4	1x1	4x4	3x5	20x1	5x4	1x1	4x4	3x5	20x1	1x1	4x4	20x1	1x1	4x4	1x1	4x4	3x5	20x1	5x4	1x1

1-20 - Blank
21-40 - Dark grey
41-60 - Grey
61-80 - Black
81-100 - Red
101-120 - Pink

Monkey

5x4	1x1	4x4	3x5	20x1	1x1	4x4	1x1	4x4	3x5	20x1	5x4	1x1	4x4	3x5	20x1	1x1	4x4	20x1	1x1	4x4	1x1	4x4	3x5	20x1	5x4	1x1
6x3	8x2	3x2	1x11	5x4	8x2	3x2	8x2	3x2	1x11	5x4	6x3	8x2	3x2	1x11	5x4	8x2	3x2	5x4	8x2	3x2	8x2	3x2	1x11	5x4	6x3	8x2
1x1	20x1	6x3	4x4	3x5	20x1	5x4	1x1	20x1	6x3	8x2	1x1	2x16	11x2	40x1	4x4	20x1	1x1	4x4	1x1	4x4	3x5	20x1	5x4	1x1	20x1	6x3
6x3	4x4	1x1	5x4	1x1	4x4	20x1	6x3	4x4	1x1	15x2	12x3	15x2	2x16	12x3	11x2	15x2	3x2	5x4	8x2	5x4	1x1	4x4	20x1	6x3	4x4	1x1
8x2	3x2	8x2	6x3	8x2	3x2	5x4	8x2	2x16	11x2	40x1	14x8	11x2	28x4	40x1	30x4	2x16	11x2	40x1	1x1	6x3	8x2	3x2	5x4	8x2	3x2	8x2
20x1	5x4	1x1	3x2	9x8	6x3	8x2	12x3	15x2	2x16	30x4	12x3	30x4	2x16	26x4	15x2	28x4	2x16	12x3	2x16	20x1	1x1	9x8	3x5	20x1	5x4	1x1
5x4	6x3	8x2	5x4	40x2	20x1	6x3	40x1	11x2	55x2	11x2	20x6	22x5	55x2	20x6	22x5	40x1	55x2	2x16	40x1	3x2	8x2	40x2	1x11	5x4	6x3	8x2
1x1	20x1	1x1	31x2	10x9	9x8	2x16	12x3	14x8	15x2	22x5	55x2	30x4	120x1	55x2	30x4	55x2	11x2	14x8	12x3	2x16	9x8	9x9	5x8	1x1	20x1	1x1
5x4	6x3	8x2	15x5	9x7	40x2	11x2	26x4	15x2	30x4	26x4	28x4	14x8	110x1	28x4	14x8	28x4	14x8	15x2	26x4	11x2	40x2	9x7	40x2	5x4	6x3	8x2
1x1	20x1	6x3	9x7	10x9	9x7	2x16	11x2	2x16	20x6	22x5	55x2	30x4	120x1	55x2	30x4	55x2	30x4	2x16	40x1	2x16	9x7	10x9	15x5	1x1	20x1	6x3
6x3	4x4	1x1	9x8	9x9	31x2	11x2	30x4	9x9	25x4	45x2	25x4	14x8	110x1	28x4	25x4	45x2	9x9	45x2	30x4	11x2	31x2	9x9	9x7	6x3	4x4	1x1
4x4	1x1	9x8	40x2	15x6	15x5	12x3	10x9	15x6	45x2	10x9	9x9	45x2	120x1	15x6	45x2	10x9	25x4	11x9	9x9	12x3	15x5	15x6	9x8	40x2	6x3	8x2
6x3	8x2	40x2	9x7	40x2	9x7	25x4	11x9	9x9	11x9	9x9	10x9	11x9	9x9	11x9	10x9	9x9	9x9	45x2	10x9	45x2	9x7	31x2	40x2	9x7	20x1	6x3
20x1	6x3	9x7	10x9	11x9	9x8	9x9	45x2	10x9	4x4	132x1	25x4	15x6	25x4	45x2	25x4	14x10	4x4	11x9	9x9	11x9	9x8	10x9	11x9	9x8	4x4	1x1
4x4	1x1	31x2	25x4	15x6	40x2	25x4	11x9	9x9	20x1	3x45	10x9	11x9	9x9	11x9	10x9	20x1	3x45	45x2	10x9	45x2	40x2	25x4	15x6	40x2	3x2	8x2
3x2	8x2	15x5	9x9	11x9	9x7	40x1	25x4	15x6	14x10	25x5	25x4	15x6	25x4	45x2	25x4	14x10	25x5	10x9	25x4	15x2	9x7	9x9	11x9	9x7	5x4	1x1
5x4	1x1	15x2	25x4	45x2	6x9	2x16	12x3	25x4	10x9	11x9	45x2	35x4	25x4	132x1	45x2	10x9	11x9	9x9	2x16	12x3	6x9	25x4	45x2	15x2	6x3	8x2
6x3	8x2	12x3	45x2	10x9	25x2	2x16	11x2	40x1	25x4	15x6	10x9	11x9	9x9	11x9	10x9	25x4	15x6	2x16	11x2	40x1	25x2	45x2	10x9	12x3	20x1	1x1
20x1	40x1	25x4	11x9	9x9	10x6	15x2	2x16	12x3	9x9	11x9	25x4	15x6	25x4	45x2	25x4	9x9	11x9	15x2	2x16	12x3	10x6	25x4	11x9	9x9	40x1	8x2
6x3	12x3	9x9	45x2	10x9	6x9	12x3	11x2	40x1	25x4	45x2	132x1	35x4	20x1	3x45	14x10	25x4	45x2	12x3	11x2	40x1	6x9	9x9	45x2	10x9	12x3	6x3
1x1	40x1	25x4	11x9	9x9	6x9	25x2	2x16	12x3	45x2	10x9	45x2	14x11	8x20	80x2	45x2	45x2	10x9	2x16	12x3	10x6	6x9	25x4	11x9	9x9	40x1	1x1
8x2	6x9	45x2	10x9	40x1	19x3	1x1	19x3	40x1	11x9	9x9	10x9	11x9	9x9	11x9	10x9	11x9	9x9	15x2	30x2	1x1	19x3	40x1	25x4	15x6	10x6	8x2
6x3	25x2	2x16	11x2	15x2	25x2	8x2	4x4	10x6	30x2	6x9	25x4	15x6	25x4	45x2	25x4	19x3	30x2	6x9	3x2	8x2	25x2	2x16	11x2	40x1	6x9	6x3
1x1	10x6	15x2	2x16	12x3	10x6	1x1	3x5	20x1	5x4	1x1	25x2	15x4	10x6	30x2	6x9	4x4	3x5	20x1	5x4	1x1	10x6	15x2	2x16	12x3	10x6	1x1
8x2	6x9	12x3	11x2	40x1	6x9	8x2	4x4	3x5	20x1	5x4	1x1	19x3	30x2	6x9	4x4	3x2	1x11	5x4	6x3	8x2	6x9	12x3	11x2	40x1	30x2	8x2
1x1	1x11	25x2	6x9	19x3	1x1	6x3	3x2	1x11	5x4	6x3	8x2	5x4	1x1	20x1	6x3	20x1	5x4	1x1	20x1	6x3	5x4	25x2	15x4	6x9	5x4	1x1
8x2	4x4	1x1	4x4	3x5	20x1	8x2	20x1	5x4	1x1	20x1	6x3	20x1	6x3	4x4	1x1	4x4	20x1	6x3	4x4	1x1	4x4	1x1	4x4	3x5	20x1	8x2
1x1	3x2	8x2	3x2	1x11	5x4	1x1	4x4	20x1	6x3	4x4	1x1	5x4	8x2	3x2	8x2	3x2	5x4	8x2	3x2	8x2	3x2	8x2	3x2	1x11	5x4	1x1
20x1	4x4	3x5	20x1	5x4	1x1	20x1	3x2	5x4	8x2	3x2	8x2	4x4	20x1	6x3	4x4	1x1	4x4	1x1	4x4	3x5	4x4	3x5	20x1	5x4	1x1	20x1
5x4	5x4	1x1	4x4	20x1	6x3	5x4	6x3	8x2	5x4	1x1	20x1	3x2	5x4	8x2	3x2	8x2	3x2	8x2	3x2	1x11	5x4	1x1	4x4	20x1	6x3	5x4

1-20 - Blank
21-40 - Brown
41-60 - Dark brown
61-80 - Light brown
81-100 - Cream
101-120 - Olive green
121-140 - Black
141-160 - Wine

Screaming Emoji

3x5	20x1	1x1	4x4	3x5	1x1	4x4	20x1	3x5	20x1	1x1	4x4	3x5	1x1	4x4	20x1	5x4	1x1	4x4	3x5	20x1	1x1	4x4	1x1
5x4	1x1	4x4	3x5	20x1	1x1	4x4	1x1	4x4	3x5	20x1	1x1	4x4	3x5	1x1	4x4	20x1	4x4	1x1	4x4	3x5	20x1	5x4	3x5
3x5	20x1	1x1	4x4	3x5	1x1	4x4	20x1	3x5	20x1	1x1	4x4	3x5	1x1	4x4	20x1	5x4	1x1	4x4	3x5	20x1	1x1	4x4	1x1
20x1	1x1	25x4	1x1	25x4	20x1	5x4	1x1	4x4	3x5	20x1	1x1	4x4	5x4	3x5	20x1	1x1	4x4	5x4	25x4	1x1	25x4	3x5	20x1
1x1	45x2	10x9	45x2	10x9	45x2	3x5	20x1	1x1	4x4	3x5	4x4	20x1	20x1	5x4	1x1	4x4	3x5	45x2	10x9	45x2	10x9	45x2	1x1
3x5	11x9	9x9	11x9	9x9	11x9	5x4	1x1	4x4	3x5	20x1	1x1	4x4	1x1	3x5	20x1	1x1	4x4	11x9	9x9	11x9	9x9	11x9	3x5
1x1	3x5	25x4	15x6	25x4	20x1	3x5	20x1	1x1	11x2	40x1	12x3	11x2	40x1	12x3	3x5	20x1	6x1	4x4	25x4	15x6	25x4	4x4	1x1
20x1	4x4	5x4	10x9	20x1	1x1	4x4	40x1	30x1	19x3	6x9	25x2	6x9	19x3	6x9	40x1	30x1	4x4	3x5	20x1	10x9	20x1	3x5	20x1
4x4	3x5	20x1	6x1	3x5	4x4	11x2	25x2	15x4	25x2	10x6	30x2	25x2	15x4	25x2	15x4	25x2	40x1	4x4	1x1	20x1	1x1	4x4	1x1
5x4	1x1	4x4	3x5	20x1	40x1	6x9	10x6	30x2	10x6	6x9	19x3	6x9	30x2	10x6	30x2	10x6	6x9	11x2	5x4	1x1	20x1	3x5	20x1
3x5	20x1	1x1	4x4	2x16	15x4	25x2	6x9	19x3	6x9	25x2	15x4	10x6	30x2	6x9	19x3	6x9	15x4	25x2	2x16	20x1	1x1	4x4	1x1
4x4	3x5	20x1	6x1	15x2	30x2	10x6	30x4	26x4	28x4	10x6	30x2	6x9	19x3	30x4	26x4	28x4	30x2	10x6	15x2	3x5	20x1	5x4	3x5
3x5	20x1	1x1	30x1	6x9	19x3	27x4	1x1	4x4	3x5	22x5	14x10	25x5	110x1	1x1	4x4	1x1	40x3	6x9	19x3	30x1	1x1	4x4	1x1
5x4	1x1	4x4	15x2	14x10	26x4	5x4	20x1	3x5	20x1	110x1	132x1	35x4	27x4	20x1	3x5	20x1	3x5	26x4	14x10	15x2	20x1	3x5	20x1
3x5	20x1	1x1	9x4	132x1	22x5	4x4	3x5	20x1	28x4	25x5	20x7	66x2	121x1	55x2	20x1	3x5	20x1	22x5	132x1	9x4	1x1	4x4	3x5
4x4	3x5	20x1	5x8	20x7	110x1	3x5	4x4	40x3	132x1	35x4	20x1	3x45	14x10	25x5	27x4	1x1	4x4	110x1	20x7	5x8	20x1	3x5	20x1
5x4	1x1	4x4	40x2	35x4	20x7	26x4	28x4	3x45	14x10	25x5	30x4	26x4	25x5	20x7	66x2	30x4	26x4	132x1	35x4	40x2	1x1	4x4	1x1
4x4	20x1	3x5	9x4	66x2	132x1	35x4	20x1	14x10	25x5	28x4	25x4	9x9	22x5	25x5	20x7	66x2	3x45	20x7	66x2	9x4	20x1	5x4	3x5
3x5	20x1	1x1	4x4	30x1	15x2	40x2	25x5	132x1	35x4	55x2	10x9	15x6	110x1	35x4	20x1	3x45	30x1	9x4	30x1	20x1	1x1	4x4	1x1
5x4	1x1	4x4	3x5	15x2	132x1	35x4	9x4	20x7	66x2	40x3	9x9	25x4	27x4	20x7	66x2	9x4	132x1	35x4	15x2	3x5	20x1	5x4	3x5
3x5	20x1	1x1	4x4	9x4	14x10	25x5	20x1	5x8	25x5	26x4	15x6	10x9	14x8	25x5	5x8	20x1	14x10	25x5	9x4	20x1	1x1	4x4	1x1
4x4	3x5	20x1	6x1	3x5	15x2	35x4	3x45	14x10	35x4	20x1	30x4	26x4	35x4	3x45	14x10	35x4	20x1	5x8	5x4	1x1	20x1	3x5	20x1
5x4	1x1	4x4	3x5	20x1	6x1	40x2	14x10	25x5	15x2	40x2	20x7	66x2	15x2	40x2	25x5	20x7	5x8	4x4	20x1	4x4	1x1	4x4	3x5
4x4	20x1	3x5	1x1	3x5	1x1	9x4	132x1	35x4	9x4	4x4	30x1	15x2	4x4	9x4	35x4	20x1	40x2	20x1	5x4	1x1	20x1	3x5	20x1
3x5	20x1	1x1	4x4	3x5	1x1	4x4	20x1	3x5	20x1	1x1	4x4	3x5	1x1	4x4	20x1	5x4	1x1	4x4	3x5	20x1	1x1	4x4	1x1
5x4	1x1	4x4	3x5	20x1	6x1	3x5	1x1	4x4	3x5	20x1	1x1	4x4	3x5	1x1	4x4	20x1	4x4	1x1	4x4	3x5	20x1	5x4	3x5
3x5	20x1	1x1	4x4	3x5	1x1	4x4	20x1	3x5	20x1	1x1	4x4	3x5	1x1	4x4	20x1	5x4	1x1	4x4	3x5	20x1	1x1	4x4	1x1

1-20 - Blank
21-40 - Navy
41-60 - Blue
61-80 - Orange
81-100 - Red
101-120 - Black
121-140 - Yellow

Quarter Moon Emoji

1x1	4x4	3x5	5x4	1x1	4x4	3x5	20x1	1x1	4x4	5x4	1x1	4x4	3x5	1x1	4x4	3x5	5x4	1x1	4x4	3x5	20x1	1x1	4x4	5x4	1x1	4x4	3x5
8x2	3x2	1x11	6x3	8x2	3x2	1x11	5x4	8x2	3x2	6x3	8x2	3x2	1x11	8x2	3x2	1x11	6x3	8x2	3x2	1x11	5x4	8x2	3x2	6x3	8x2	3x2	1x11
6x3	20x1	8x2	10x2	6x3	20x1	8x2	3x2	6x3	20x1	10x2	6x3	20x1	8x2	6x3	20x1	8x2	10x2	6x3	20x1	8x2	3x2	6x3	20x1	10x2	6x3	20x1	8x2
3x5	1x1	5x4	30x2	3x5	1x1	5x4	4x4	3x5	1x1	4x4	3x5	1x1	5x4	3x5	1x1	5x4	4x4	3x5	1x1	5x4	4x4	3x5	1x1	4x4	3x5	1x1	5x4
1x11	8x2	3x2	6x9	7x2	20x1	6x3	7x11	15x5	40x2	20x4	8x9	3x25	9x7	7x2	10x2	8x2	1x11	7x2	10x2	8x2	6x3	7x2	10x2	1x11	7x2	10x2	8x2
8x2	6x3	20x3	7x8	5x12	3x5	5x4	4x4	40x2	10x5	5x9	30x2	6x9	3x16	15x5	40x2	1x1	4x4	3x5	5x4	8x3	40x1	9x4	8x3	1x1	5x4	7x2	20x1
5x4	10x5	5x9	30x2	6x9	3x16	7x2	20x1	6x3	7x11	6x9	7x8	5x12	20x3	7x8	5x12	7x11	15x5	4x4	6x4	7x5	20x2	6x4	7x5	8x3	3x5	1x1	4x4
8x2	4x4	20x3	7x8	5x12	20x1	6x3	8x2	7x2	20x1	16x4	3x16	6x9	3x16	3x16	5x12	7x8	5x12	9x7	17x2	20x2	8x3	17x2	20x2	17x2	20x2	3x5	7x2
20x1	5x4	7x2	3x16	20x1	4x4	3x5	20x1	1x1	4x4	15x5	5x12	40x2	20x4	5x12	20x3	3x16	5x12	7x8	7x11	8x3	40x1	9x4	8x3	9x4	8x3	17x2	1x1
4x4	3x5	1x1	5x12	4x4	3x2	1x11	5x4	8x2	3x2	20x1	3x25	6x9	3x16	5x9	30x2	5x12	20x3	3x16	30x2	16x4	5x4	7x2	20x1	6x3	8x2	7x2	20x1
7x2	8x2	3x2	1x11	5x4	20x1	8x2	3x2	6x3	20x1	4x4	9x7	5x12	15x5	7x11	20x3	5x9	30x2	5x12	7x8	15x5	3x5	1x1	4x4	3x5	20x1	1x1	4x4
1x1	6x3	20x1	8x2	3x2	1x1	5x4	4x4	3x5	1x1	3x2	40x2	9x7	10x5	5x9	30x2	16x4	5x12	7x8	5x12	30x2	3x25	8x2	3x2	1x11	5x4	8x2	3x2
20x1	3x5	5x4	15x2	40x1	7x5	15x2	40x1	7x2	8x2	20x1	15x5	7x8	5x12	12x10	15x7	6x9	9x7	3x16	5x12	6x9	9x7	6x3	20x1	8x2	3x2	6x3	20x1
4x4	1x1	7x5	6x4	7x5	20x2	6x4	7x5	8x3	6x3	1x1	3x25	3x16	5x12	20x6	25x4	3x2	40x2	5x12	20x3	7x8	40x2	3x5	1x1	5x4	4x4	3x5	1x1
3x2	15x2	20x2	17x2	20x2	8x3	17x2	20x2	17x2	20x2	16x4	6x9	10x5	5x9	50x2	6x3	20x1	10x5	5x9	30x2	6x9	3x16	16x4	10x2	8x2	6x3	7x2	10x2
40x1	6x4	8x3	9x4	8x3	40x1	9x4	8x3	9x4	8x3	15x5	7x8	5x12	20x3	7x8	5x12	30x2	6x9	30x2	6x9	15x4	15x4	20x4	4x4	5x4	1x1	4x4	3x5
1x1	3x2	6x3	20x1	10x2	6x3	20x1	8x2	3x5	20x4	5x12	30x2	6x9	3x16	3x16	5x12	6x9	10x5	6x9	10x5	5x9	30x2	15x5	3x2	6x3	8x2	3x2	1x11
10x2	4x4	3x5	1x1	4x4	3x5	1x1	5x4	3x25	20x3	7x8	5x12	40x2	20x4	5x12	20x3	5x12	20x3	7x8	5x12	20x3	7x8	3x25	20x1	10x2	6x3	20x1	8x2
3x5	6x3	7x2	10x2	1x11	7x2	10x2	8x2	1x1	3x2	6x3	16x4	6x9	3x16	5x9	30x2	10x5	5x9	30x2	6x9	3x16	3x16	7x11	1x1	4x4	3x5	1x1	5x4
1x11	10x2	6x3	20x1	8x2	30x2	6x3	10x2	1x11	7x2	10x2	10x5	5x9	30x2	6x9	3x16	3x16	20x3	7x8	15x4	30x2	9x7	6x3	10x2	1x11	7x2	10x2	8x2
8x2	4x4	3x5	1x1	5x4	6x9	3x5	1x1	5x4	1x1	4x4	15x5	40x2	20x4	8x9	3x25	5x12	6x9	3x16	5x12	6x9	16x4	3x5	1x1	5x4	1x1	4x4	3x5
5x4	6x3	20x1	8x2	20x3	7x8	5x12	6x3	10x2	8x2	9x7	5x9	20x3	5x12	3x16	5x12	6x9	7x8	5x12	20x3	7x8	15x5	7x2	20x1	30x2	8x2	3x2	1x11
8x2	3x5	1x1	10x5	5x9	30x2	6x9	3x16	6x3	10x2	3x2	7x11	15x5	20x3	5x12	20x3	7x8	6x9	7x8	5x12	20x4	5x4	1x1	4x4	6x9	8x2	7x2	20x1
3x5	6x3	8x2	7x2	20x3	7x8	5x12	4x4	3x5	1x1	20x4	30x2	6x9	30x2	5x9	30x2	6x9	15x4	3x16	5x12	3x25	1x1	8x2	20x3	7x8	5x12	5x4	4x4
3x2	1x1	5x4	1x1	6x3	3x16	4x4	8x2	7x2	20x1	3x25	6x9	10x5	6x9	30x2	6x9	15x4	5x9	15x4	8x9	6x3	8x2	10x5	5x9	30x2	6x9	3x16	3x2
5x4	1x11	6x3	8x2	3x5	5x12	3x2	6x3	8x2	9x7	7x8	5x12	20x3	7x8	6x9	10x5	5x9	20x3	9x7	8x2	7x2	3x2	6x3	20x3	7x8	5x12	6x3	5x4
1x1	3x5	1x1	5x4	4x4	3x5	1x1	10x2	6x3	40x2	3x16	10x5	5x9	30x2	10x5	5x9	8x9	3x25	3x5	1x1	5x4	4x4	3x5	1x1	3x16	4x4	3x5	1x1
10x2	7x2	20x1	6x3	8x2	7x2	20x1	3x2	16x4	15x4	10x5	30x2	6x9	3x16	40x2	20x4	6x3	8x2	7x2	20x1	6x3	8x2	7x2	20x1	5x12	1x11	7x2	10x2
3x5	1x1	4x4	3x5	20x1	1x1	4x4	7x11	15x5	40x2	20x4	8x9	3x25	9x7	1x1	4x4	3x5	5x4	1x1	4x4	3x5	20x1	1x1	4x4	5x4	1x1	4x4	3x5
1x11	8x2	3x2	1x11	5x4	8x2	3x2	5x4	8x2	3x2	6x3	8x2	3x2	1x11	8x2	3x2	1x11	6x3	8x2	3x2	1x11	5x4	8x2	3x2	6x3	8x2	3x2	1x11
8x2	6x3	20x1	8x2	3x2	6x3	20x1	3x2	6x3	20x1	10x2	6x3	20x1	8x2	6x3	20x1	8x2	10x2	6x3	20x1	8x2	3x2	6x3	20x1	10x2	6x3	20x1	8x2
5x4	3x5	1x1	5x4	4x4	3x5	1x1	4x4	3x5	1x1	4x4	3x5	1x1	5x4	3x5	1x1	5x4	4x4	3x5	1x1	5x4	4x4	3x5	1x1	4x4	3x5	1x1	5x4
8x2	7x2	10x2	8x2	6x3	7x2	10x2	6x3	7x2	10x2	1x11	7x2	10x2	8x2	7x2	10x2	8x2	1x11	7x2	10x2	8x2	6x3	7x2	10x2	1x11	7x2	10x2	8x2

1-20 - Blank
21-40 - Blue
41-60 - Yellow
61-80 - Orange
81-100 - Grey
101-120 - Black

Blowing a Kiss Emoji

3x5	20x1	1x1	4x4	3x5	1x1	4x4	20x1	5x4	1x1	4x4	3x5	20x1	1x1	4x4	1x1	3x5	20x1	1x1	4x4	3x5	1x1	4x4	20x1
5x4	1x1	4x4	3x5	20x1	1x1	4x4	1x1	4x4	3x5	20x1	1x1	4x4	3x5	1x1	4x4	20x1	4x4	1x1	4x4	3x5	20x1	5x4	1x1
4x4	3x5	20x1	1x1	4x4	5x4	1x1	20x1	40x3	55x2	30x4	120x1	14x8	110x1	3x5	1x1	5x4	1x1	4x4	3x5	20x1	1x1	4x4	3x5
3x5	1x1	4x4	20x1	4x4	1x1	40x3	55x2	15x2	20x2	15x2	10x4	20x2	15x2	27x4	26x4	4x4	3x5	20x1	1x1	4x4	5x4	1x1	20x1
4x4	1x1	3x5	1x1	28x4	120x1	12x3	11x2	40x1	11x2	40x1	12x3	11x2	40x1	11x2	40x1	14x8	110x1	1x1	4x4	3x5	1x1	5x4	4x4
1x1	4x4	20x1	22x5	3x10	7x4	28x4	14x8	110x1	12x2	5x8	30x1	12x2	5x8	12x2	5x8	30x1	12x2	26x4	1x1	4x4	3x5	20x1	5x4
20x1	5x4	14x8	2x16	20x2	40x3	55x2	30x4	120x1	3x10	7x4	2x16	3x10	7x4	3x10	7x4	2x16	3x10	7x4	28x4	20x1	5x4	1x1	4x4
1x1	55x2	15x2	40x1	120x1	15x8	2x16	3x10	7x4	20x2	15x2	10x4	20x2	15x2	27x4	26x4	28x4	7x4	12x3	11x2	26x4	4x4	3x5	20x1
20x1	40x3	40x1	27x4	22x5	11x2	40x1	26x4	28x4	11x2	40x1	12x3	11x2	40x1	11x2	40x1	40x3	26x4	20x2	15x2	22x5	5x4	1x1	4x4
28x4	12x3	20x2	55x2	15x2	10x4	27x4	22x5	55x2	10x4	20x2	15x2	10x4	20x2	15x2	10x4	20x2	15x2	30x4	15x2	10x4	28x4	5x4	1x1
55x2	30x1	110x1	10x4	20x2	15x2	14x8	110x1	40x3	12x3	11x2	40x1	30x4	26x4	28x4	14x8	110x1	12x2	5x8	10x4	20x2	55x2	4x4	3x5
40x3	20x2	15x2	12x3	11x2	40x1	30x4	120x1	15x8	30x1	12x2	5x8	20x6	22x5	55x2	30x4	120x1	3x10	7x4	12x3	11x2	40x3	1x1	20x1
26x4	11x2	40x1	30x1	12x2	5x8	20x6	12x10	52x2	2x16	3x10	7x4	10x4	20x2	15x2	10x4	20x2	15x2	10x4	20x2	15x2	15x8	5x4	4x4
22x5	10x4	20x2	15x2	10x4	20x2	15x2	10x4	20x2	15x2	26x4	28x4	12x3	11x2	40x1	12x3	11x2	40x1	12x3	11x2	40x1	52x2	20x1	5x4
110x1	12x3	11x2	40x1	12x3	11x2	40x1	12x3	11x2	40x1	22x5	55x2	26x4	10x4	20x2	15x2	40x2	30x1	5x8	20x2	15x2	30x1	9x4	4x4
27x4	30x1	12x2	5x8	30x1	12x2	5x8	30x1	12x2	5x8	10x4	20x2	22x5	30x4	11x2	5x8	25x4	15x4	25x2	40x2	25x2	15x4	25x2	30x1
14x8	2x16	3x10	7x4	2x16	3x10	7x4	2x16	3x10	7x4	12x3	11x2	110x1	20x6	15x2	40x2	10x9	30x2	10x6	9x4	10x6	30x2	10x6	15x2
4x4	15x8	30x1	15x2	10x4	20x2	15x2	10x4	20x2	15x2	11x2	26x4	120x1	11x2	40x1	9x4	9x9	19x3	6x9	25x2	6x9	19x3	6x9	9x4
1x1	52x2	2x16	40x1	12x3	11x2	40x1	12x3	11x2	40x1	12x2	5x8	12x10	15x8	2x16	3x10	15x2	15x6	30x2	10x6	30x2	10x6	40x2	1x1
1x1	4x4	15x8	5x8	30x1	12x2	5x8	30x1	12x2	5x8	3x10	7x4	120x1	52x2	10x4	20x2	40x1	30x1	19x3	6x9	25x2	15x2	4x4	3x5
4x4	3x5	52x2	7x4	2x16	3x10	7x4	2x16	3x10	7x4	27x4	22x5	12x10	15x2	12x3	11x2	5x8	3x10	40x2	15x4	9x4	4x4	3x5	20x1
20x1	1x1	4x4	12x10	52x2	5x8	30x1	12x2	7x4	3x10	14x8	110x1	11x2	40x1	30x1	12x2	7x4	27x4	22x5	15x2	5x4	3x5	20x1	1x1
1x1	3x5	1x1	4x4	20x1	22x5	7x4	2x16	5x8	30x1	12x2	5x8	12x2	5x8	2x16	3x10	12x10	1x1	4x4	3x5	20x1	4x4	1x1	3x5
4x4	3x5	20x1	5x4	1x1	3x5	14x8	110x1	7x4	2x16	3x10	7x4	3x10	7x4	14x8	110x1	3x5	20x1	1x1	4x4	3x5	1x1	4x4	20x1
3x5	20x1	1x1	4x4	3x5	20x1	5x4	20x1	20x6	12x10	52x2	30x4	120x1	15x8	5x4	1x1	20x1	4x4	1x1	4x4	3x5	20x1	5x4	1x1
5x4	1x1	4x4	3x5	20x1	1x1	4x4	3x5	4x4	3x5	20x1	1x1	4x4	3x5	4x4	3x5	5x4	1x1	4x4	3x5	20x1	1x1	4x4	3x5
4x4	3x5	20x1	1x1	4x4	5x4	1x1	5x4	20x1	1x1	4x4	5x4	1x1	20x1	1x1	20x1	4x4	3x5	20x1	1x1	4x4	5x4	1x1	20x1

1-20 - Blank
21-40 - Yellow
41-60 - Red
61-80 - Dark red
81-100 - Pink
101-120 - Black

Tears of Joy Emoji

6x3	8x2	6x3	8x2	4x4	3x5	1x1	8x2	6x3	3x5	1x1	5x4	8x2	4x4	3x5	1x1	5x4	4x4	3x5	20x1	4x4	20x1	6x3	4x4	20x1	6x3	8x2	6x3
3x5	6x3	8x2	70x2	14x9	70x2	14x9	6x3	8x2	7x2	10x2	8x2	20x1	1x11	7x2	10x2	8x2	3x2	1x11	5x4	6x3	70x2	3x5	70x2	14x9	3x5	6x3	8x2
1x1	5x4	31x4	35x4	2x70	35x4	2x70	31x4	20x1	7x2	20x1	6x3	4x4	8x2	7x2	20x1	6x3	10x2	8x2	6x3	31x4	35x4	2x70	35x4	2x70	31x4	3x5	20x1
10x2	35x4	2x70	65x2	42x3	65x2	42x3	2x70	35x4	1x1	4x4	3x5	6x3	5x4	1x1	4x4	3x5	5x4	4x4	35x4	2x70	65x2	42x3	65x2	42x3	2x70	35x4	5x4
3x5	1x1	8x2	6x3	7x2	20x1	6x3	8x2	4x4	3x5	1x1	15x4	10x5	5x9	30x2	6x9	3x16	8x2	6x3	7x2	20x1	6x3	8x2	4x4	3x5	1x1	5x4	4x4
6x3	3x5	1x1	5x4	8x2	4x4	8x2	7x2	10x2	5x9	30x2	6x9	40x2	1x70	20x4	8x9	15x4	10x5	5x9	1x1	4x4	3x5	20x1	1x11	7x2	10x2	8x2	6x3
8x2	7x2	10x2	8x2	20x1	1x11	4x4	30x2	6x9	3x16	3x25	9x7	16x4	8x9	3x25	9x7	20x4	40x2	30x2	6x9	3x16	5x4	4x4	8x2	7x2	20x1	6x3	8x2
20x1	7x2	20x1	6x3	4x4	8x2	3x16	5x12	16x4	8x9	9x7	16x4	8x9	3x25	9x7	16x4	8x9	3x25	9x7	8x9	3x16	5x12	6x3	5x4	1x1	4x4	3x5	20x1
5x4	8x2	6x3	7x2	20x1	30x2	1x70	20x4	40x2	1x70	8x9	40x2	1x70	20x4	8x9	40x2	3x25	9x7	16x4	3x25	9x7	16x4	15x4	6x3	8x2	3x2	1x11	5x4
6x3	7x2	20x1	6x3	5x9	8x9	40x2	1x70	8x9	40x2	20x4	8x9	40x2	1x70	20x4	8x9	20x4	8x9	40x2	40x2	1x70	20x4	8x9	3x16	7x2	10x2	8x2	6x3
3x5	8x2	4x4	15x4	3x16	9x7	16x4	8x9	9x7	16x4	3x25	9x7	16x4	8x9	3x25	9x7	1x70	20x4	8x9	16x4	8x9	3x25	9x7	5x12	15x4	1x1	4x4	3x5
7x2	20x1	1x11	20x3	9x7	16x4	8x9	3x25	16x4	8x9	9x7	16x4	8x9	3x25	9x7	16x4	8x9	40x2	1x70	8x9	3x25	9x7	16x4	40x2	20x3	10x2	1x11	7x2
8x2	1x1	5x12	3x16	20x4	8x9	40x2	1x70	8x9	40x2	20x4	8x9	40x2	1x70	20x4	8x9	40x2	16x4	8x9	1x70	20x4	8x9	40x2	16x4	3x16	5x12	3x2	8x2
6x3	3x5	30x2	3x25	40x2	1x70	9x4	7x5	15x2	16x4	40x2	1x70	16x4	8x9	3x25	9x7	20x4	40x2	1x70	6x4	40x1	9x4	16x4	8x9	40x2	30x2	20x1	6x3
3x5	3x16	20x3	9x7	8x9	20x2	8x3	40x2	1x70	20x4	8x9	16x4	8x9	3x25	9x7	16x4	8x9	3x25	9x7	20x4	40x2	20x2	8x3	1x70	8x9	20x3	3x16	3x5
4x4	15x4	9x7	8x9	40x1	9x4	20x4	40x1	17x2	20x2	8x3	40x2	1x70	20x4	8x9	40x2	16x4	17x2	20x2	8x3	17x2	8x9	6x4	7x5	20x4	8x9	15x4	4x4
8x2	20x3	16x4	20x4	15x2	8x9	7x5	40x3	40x1	9x4	7x5	15x2	40x2	1x70	20x4	8x9	6x4	40x1	9x4	7x5	40x3	6x4	9x7	17x2	3x25	9x7	20x3	8x2
20x1	3x16	40x2	3x25	40x2	1x70	15x7	12x10	40x2	16x4	8x9	8x3	16x4	8x9	3x25	9x7	17x2	40x2	16x4	8x9	12x10	15x7	16x4	3x25	9x7	16x4	3x16	20x1
4x4	5x12	8x9	9x7	40x3	20x6	50x2	20x6	20x4	40x2	1x70	16x4	8x9	3x25	9x7	16x4	3x25	20x4	40x2	1x70	20x6	40x2	40x3	20x6	8x9	40x2	5x12	4x4
3x2	30x2	15x4	20x6	25x4	25x4	9x10	40x3	6x4	7x5	20x4	40x2	1x70	20x4	8x9	40x2	16x4	8x9	20x2	8x3	40x3	25x4	25x4	9x10	40x3	15x4	30x2	3x2
8x2	20x4	15x7	40x2	50x2	40x2	50x2	12x10	1x1	5x4	40x1	17x2	20x2	8x3	6x4	7x5	20x2	9x4	5x4	4x4	12x10	50x2	40x2	50x2	40x2	15x7	8x9	8x2
6x3	70x2	14x9	50x2	9x10	50x2	9x10	20x6	40x1	1x11	7x2	6x3	10x2	7x2	10x2	1x11	7x2	1x11	7x2	17x2	20x6	9x10	50x2	9x10	25x4	70x2	14x9	6x3
3x5	35x4	2x70	31x4	50x2	40x2	40x3	7x5	7x20	15x2	40x1	7x5	15x2	40x1	9x4	8x3	40x1	9x4	8x3	7x20	6x4	40x3	9x10	40x2	2x70	35x4	2x70	3x5
7x2	65x2	42x3	2x70	70x2	14x9	15x7	20x2	14x10	65x2	42x3	21x6	7x20	42x3	21x6	7x20	42x3	65x2	42x3	14x10	17x2	15x7	2x70	65x2	42x3	65x2	42x3	7x2
6x3	4x4	12x10	15x7	40x3	20x6	40x2	1x70	8x3	7x20	14x10	65x2	14x10	7x20	65x2	14x10	7x20	7x20	14x10	7x5	40x2	1x70	12x10	15x7	40x3	20x6	5x4	4x4
4x4	3x5	1x1	5x4	4x4	5x9	16x4	8x9	20x4	6x4	7x5	7x20	42x3	14x10	7x20	42x3	14x10	20x2	8x3	40x2	16x4	8x9	10x5	3x2	8x2	3x2	6x3	8x2
1x11	7x2	10x2	8x2	6x3	1x1	15x4	10x5	7x11	15x5	40x2	17x2	20x2	8x3	6x4	7x5	20x2	7x11	15x5	40x2	20x3	7x8	8x2	20x1	6x3	8x2	7x2	20x1
8x2	7x2	20x1	6x3	8x2	7x2	20x1	20x3	7x8	5x12	16x4	7x11	40x2	1x70	20x4	8x9	3x25	20x4	30x2	6x9	3x16	20x1	5x4	4x4	3x5	20x1	1x1	4x4
5x4	1x1	4x4	3x5	20x1	1x1	4x4	1x1	4x4	30x2	6x9	3x16	16x4	8x9	3x25	9x7	15x4	10x5	5x9	8x2	7x2	4x4	6x3	3x2	1x11	5x4	8x2	3x2
6x3	8x2	3x2	1x11	5x4	8x2	3x2	8x2	3x2	6x3	8x2	15x4	10x5	5x9	30x2	6x9	3x16	6x3	8x2	3x2	1x11	5x4	8x2	3x2	8x2	3x2	6x3	8x2
10x2	6x3	20x1	8x2	3x2	6x3	20x1	6x3	20x1	10x2	6x3	3x2	20x1	6x3	20x1	10x2	6x3	10x2	6x3	20x1	8x2	3x2	6x3	20x1	6x3	20x1	10x2	6x3
4x4	3x5	1x1	5x4	4x4	3x5	1x1	3x5	1x1	4x4	3x5	4x4	1x1	3x5	1x1	4x4	3x5	4x4	3x5	1x1	5x4	4x4	3x5	1x1	3x5	1x1	4x4	3x5
1x11	7x2	10x2	8x2	6x3	7x2	10x2	7x2	10x2	1x11	7x2	6x3	10x2	7x2	10x2	1x11	7x2	1x11	7x2	10x2	8x2	6x3	7x2	10x2	7x2	10x2	1x11	7x2

1-20 - Blank
21-40 - Brown
41-60 - Orange
61-80 - Yellow
81-100 - Indigo
101-120 - Navy
121-140 - Blue
141-160 - Red

MAZES

Help these emojis find their emoji friends by finding the way through these mazes!

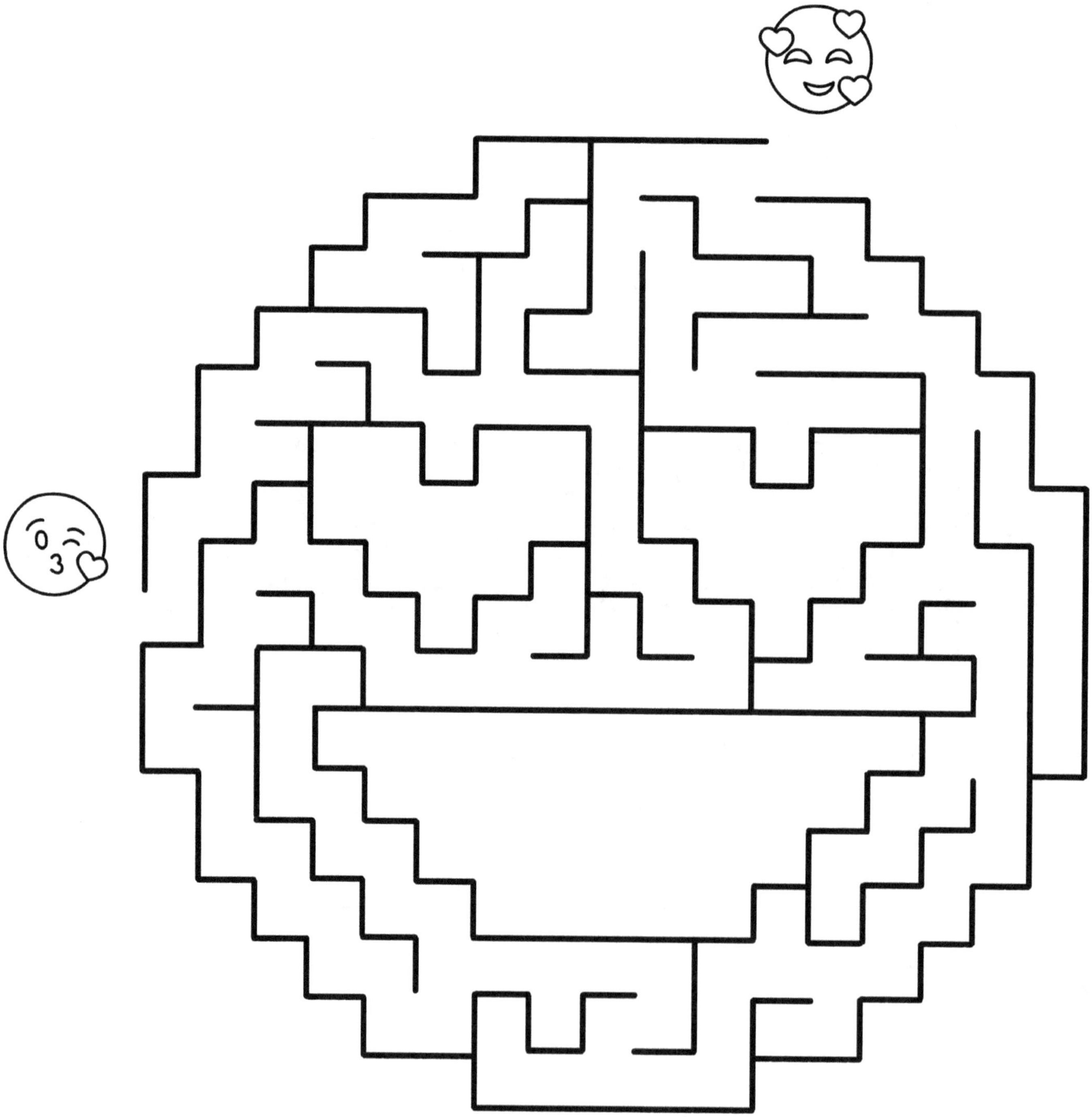

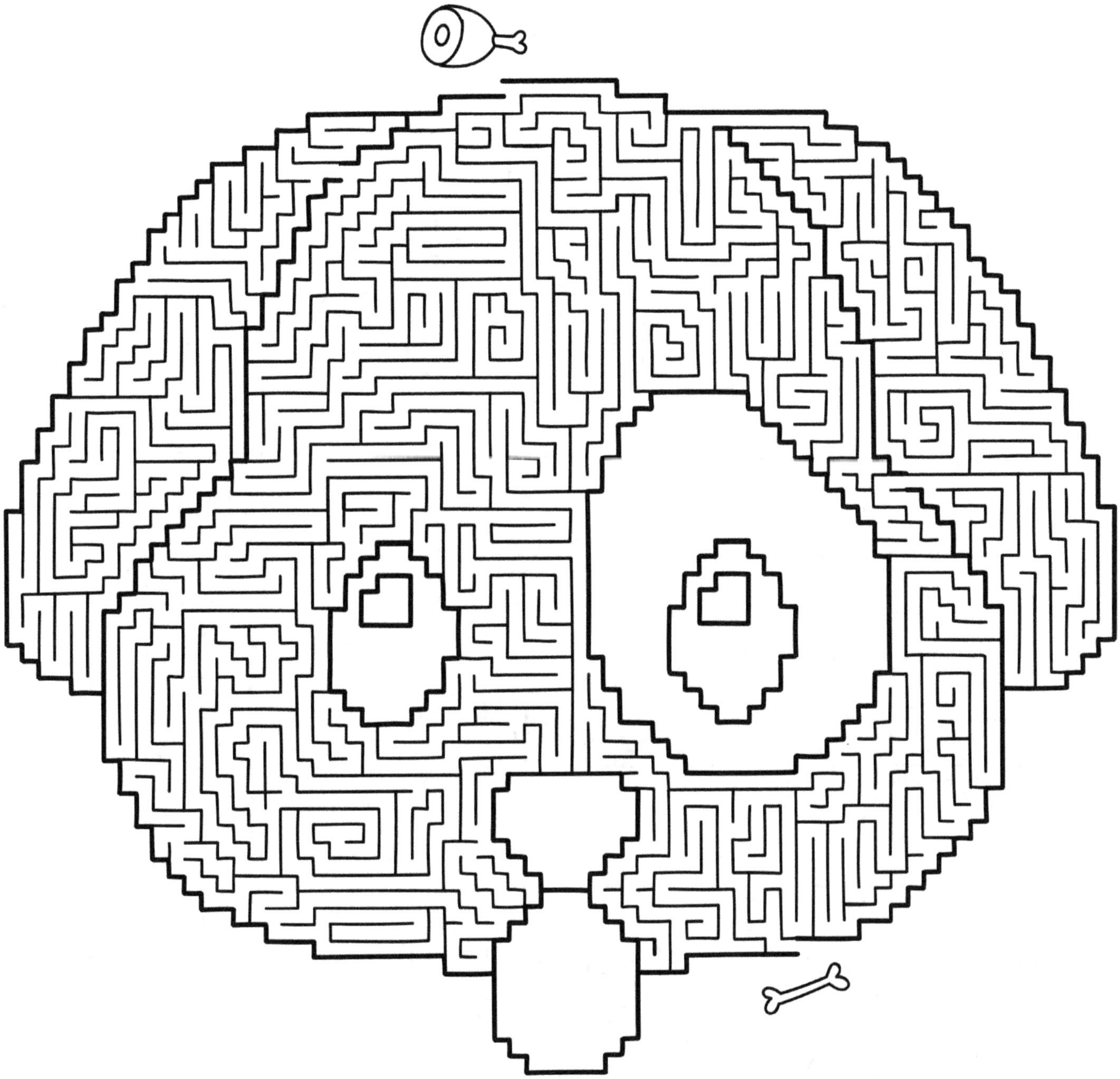

SPOT-THE-DIFFERENCE

Spot the differences!

There are 10 differences in the pictures below. Can you find them all?

There are 11 differences in the pictures below. Can you find them all?

There are 15 differences in the pictures below. Can you find them all?

There are 10 differences in the pictures below. Can you find them all?

There are 11 differences in the pictures below. Can you find them all?

FIND THE EMOJIS

These emojis have hidden themselves inside these pictures. Can you find them all?

Find these emojis!

Find these emojis!

Find these emojis!

Find these emojis! 

Find these emojis!

DECIPHER THE MEANING

Find the meaning of these emojis! Use the scrambled letters below the emojis (there are some extra letters).

1

T D S G R N A F P A E R N Q

2

M N F A E Z R D

3

O D O F Z S C T A S

4

Y I L A D O E A F M

5

U G H O L F A D

6

E M I S T C A R F

7

K O N U W F N D F N

8

V E S T O L I W

9

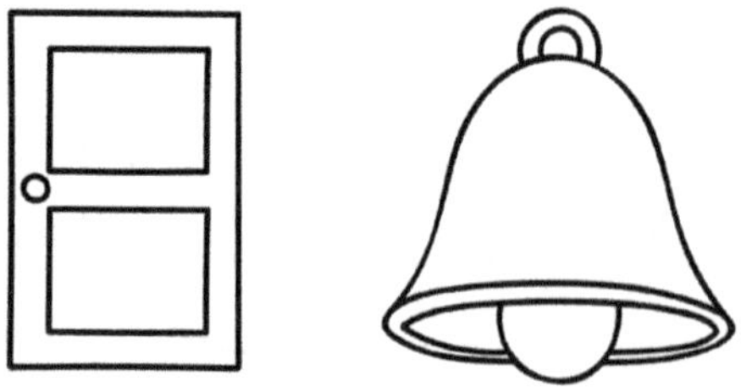

L E L B R O D O S A T

10

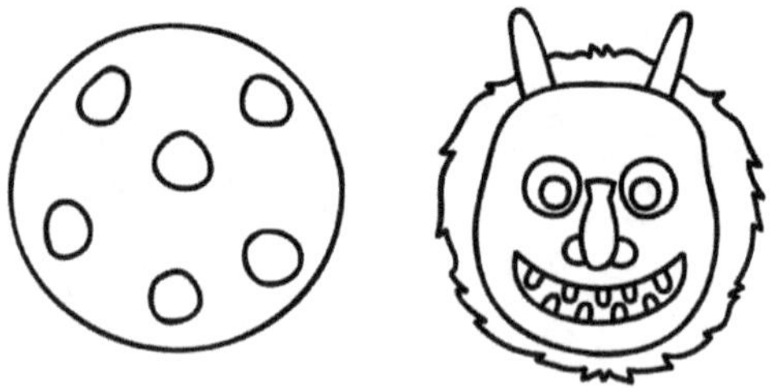

R E T S O M N O O I E C K Z A

11

R A T Y P K O C C L I T A R D

12

S E H U O I W F E E T

13

K B N A I G P Y G X C V

14

H W A S A R C A Z

15

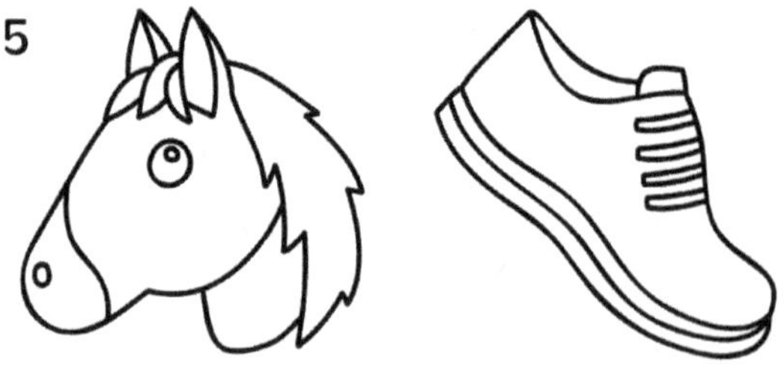

H S E E R H O S O R T

16

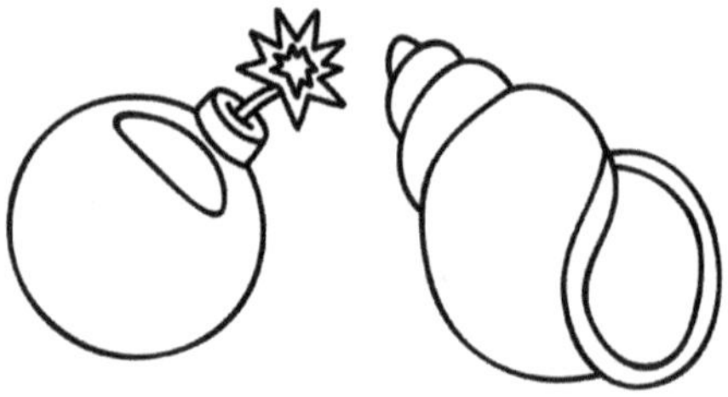

L L H S E O M B B S T

17

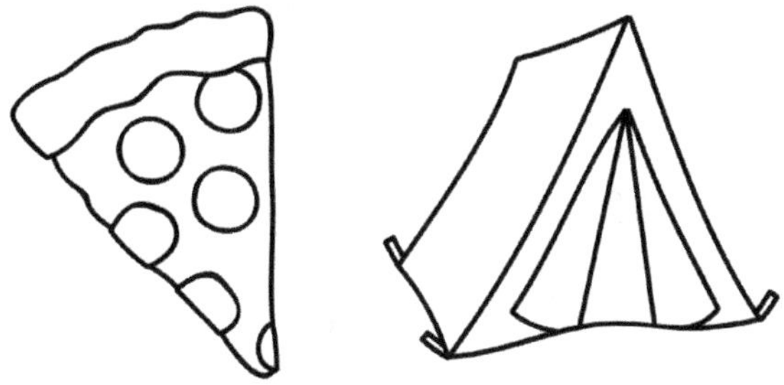

Z A Z I U H P T A C O

18

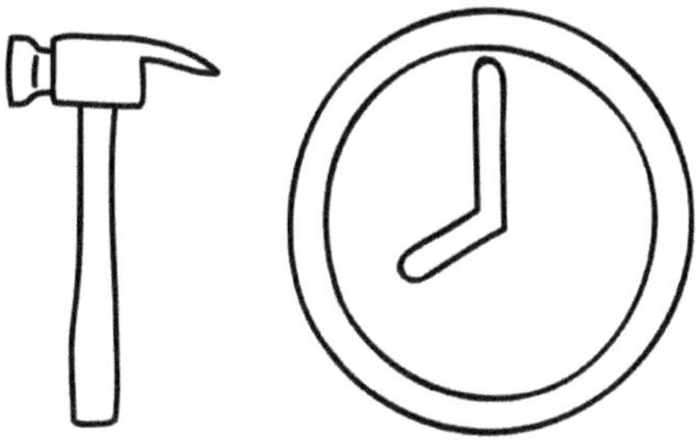

M E T I R E A M E S M H

19

S E O M N I F I G N X N I D G

20

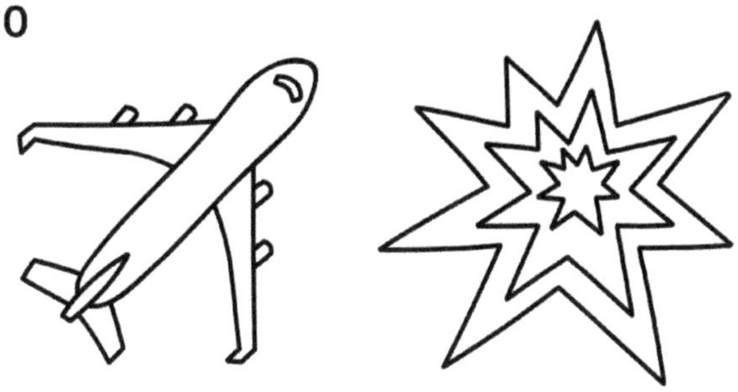

S U H C R U A P E L A N

21

P U N E S E V K A R

22

D A N H C P I S I F H S A K

23

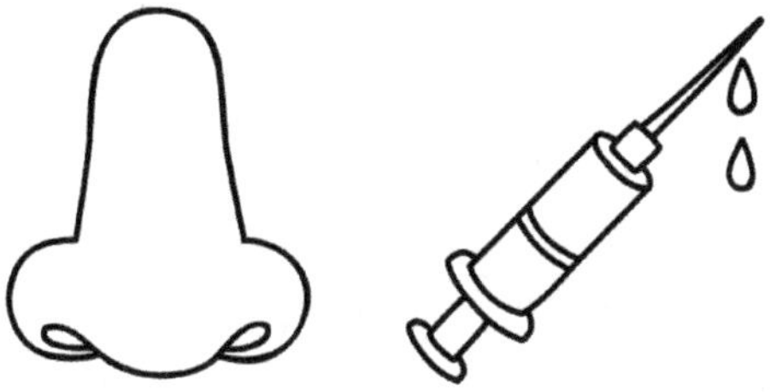

D E E N S E O B L E R S

24

D A E T R S H F O Q E E U N

25

U U O S T M R E N D R T H

26

T E T L O B B Y A B S W

27

K Y H S R U C C Y D N A A

28

Q S T S A M C H R S Y I

29

A N A M A T C W O O

30

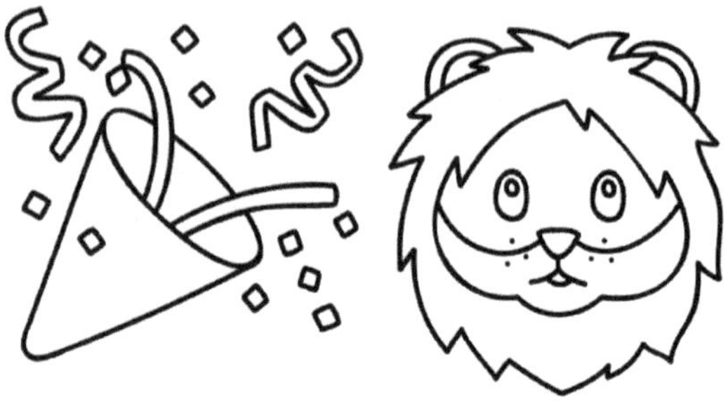

Y Z E I N A L A M R A P T

31

S O O H P T I M Y L A F A R

32

G R I B S R A M E L Y N N

33

K D R S A T S Y U C L K

34

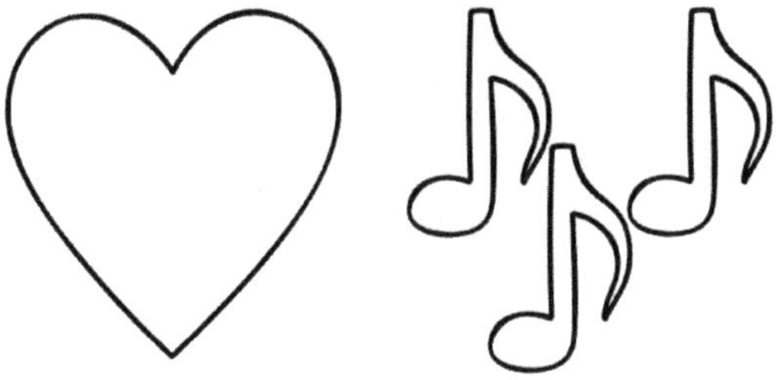

G O N G S E O L V W

35

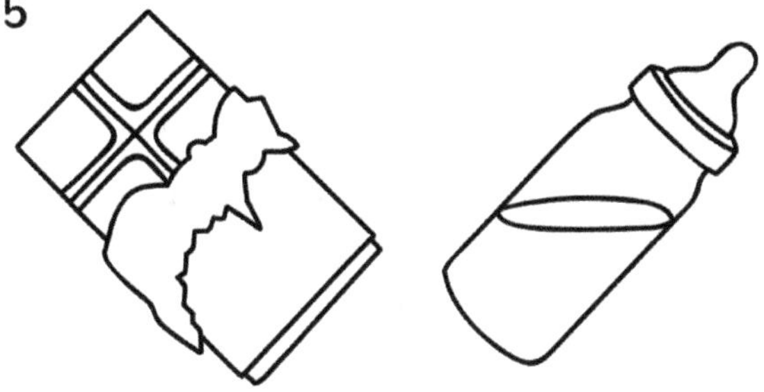

L I O T E A L H C C O S J K M

36

S T R A H Y R O P E R T G

37

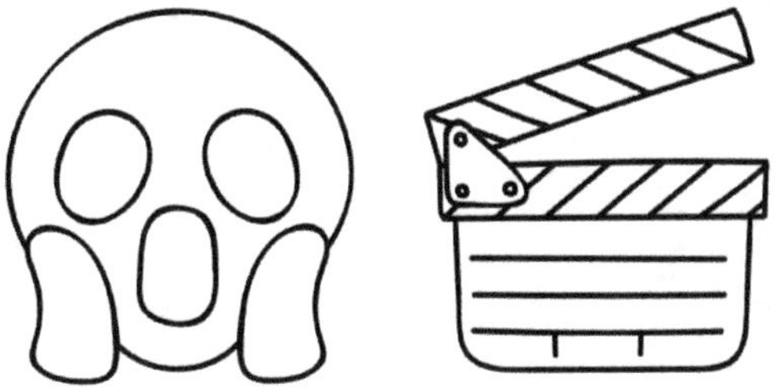

K Y R S A C I E O M V P W

38

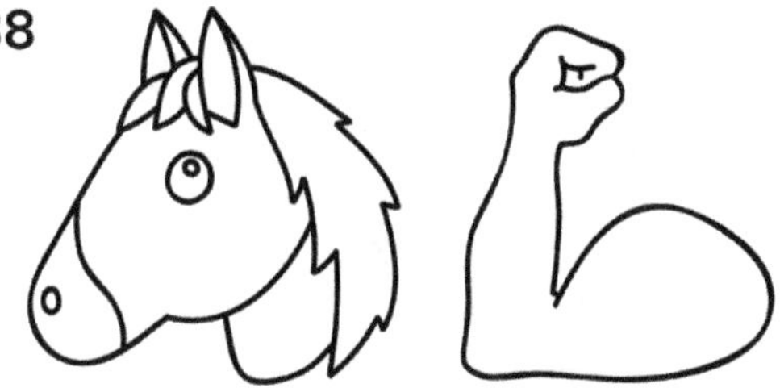

R R Z O R H E E W O P S

39

S R A G O D O O F D

40

R M T H O O R A R B

41

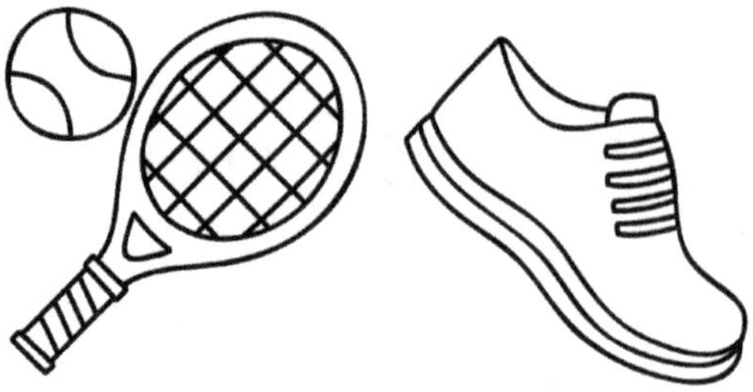

T P O N E N S S I E O H S R

42

S H C K C O A T I L P I M R

43

O O C Q K E I N U T E R O F S

44

E S U O H T I H G L Q W

45

M A R T S O N S H O N I G T

46

A S C T H S I F A S

47

F C I C E N I S E O K C R E T

48

M E E T F A H Y P Y P

49

E S S A L G U G S A N S

50

O I O K L W M A N Z

51

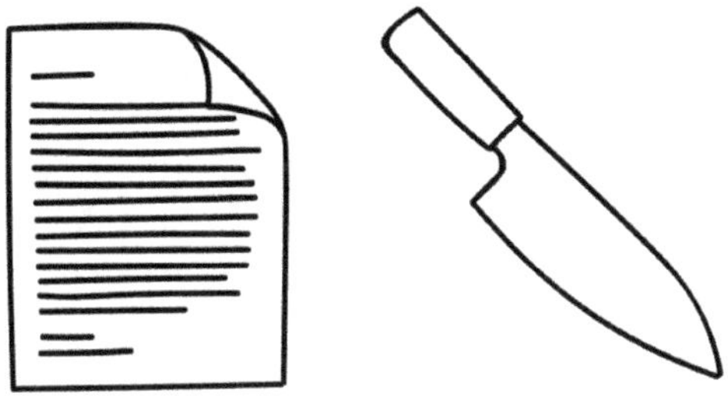

A P E P U T C W R

52

A O R Y T M S O E L V

53

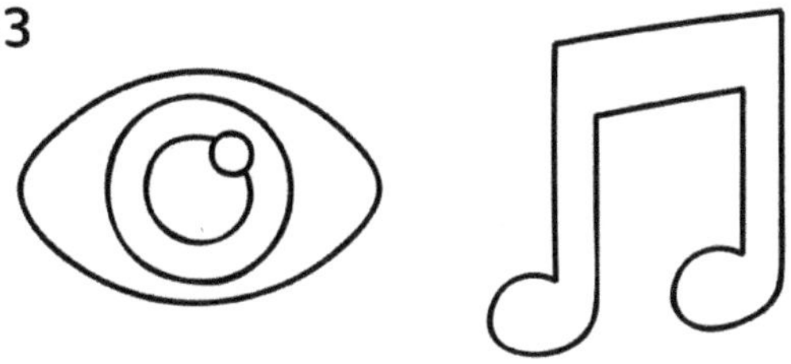

E R S N I T M K U

54

R I F R E M A L R A S

55

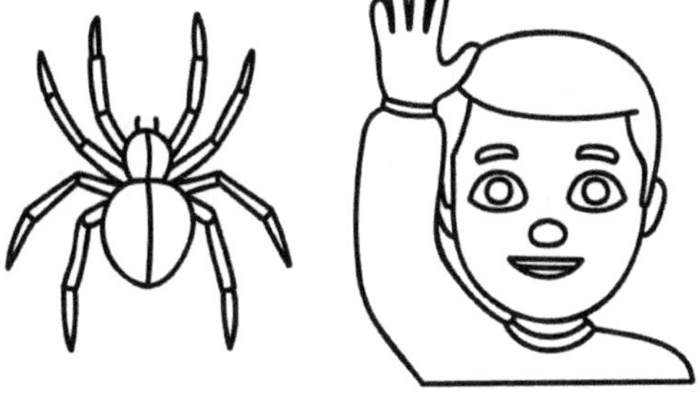

G I E R P D S A M N O

56

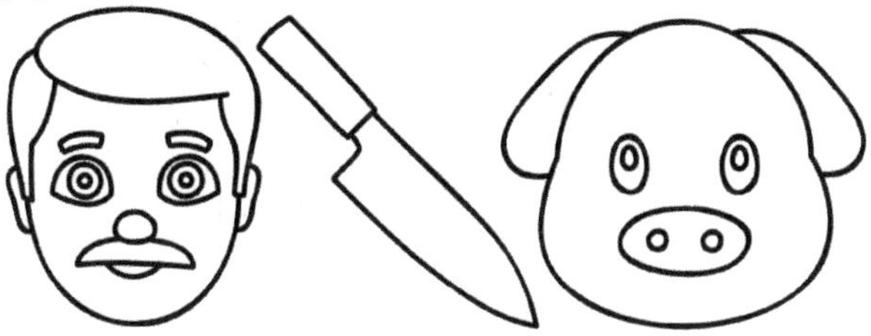

E R H T V C U S D B

57

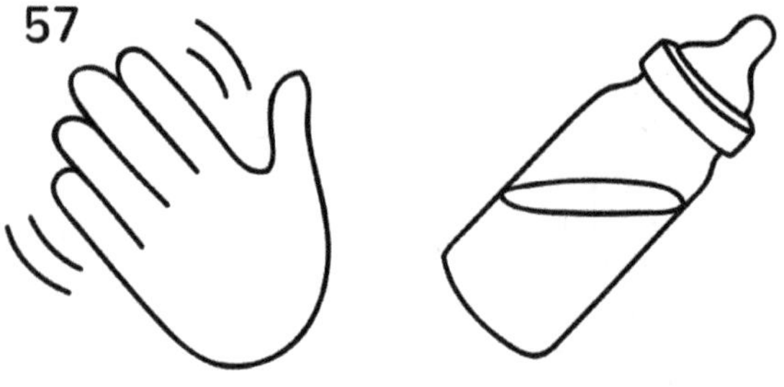

E K O H A S L I P M S K

58

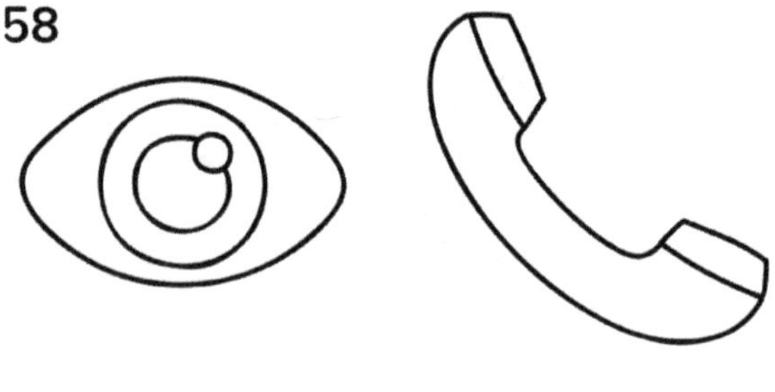

E N E I O P A H Q

59

T E T O L E V L R E S

60

A C Y H W E T A G O D

61

I F U G S H R A T A D

62

K I U B R E G R G N Z W

63

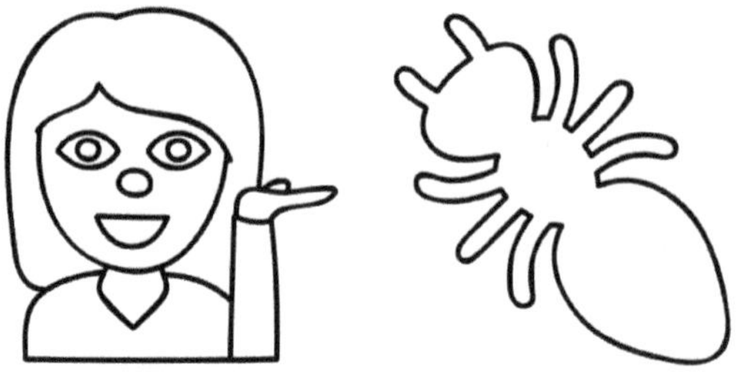

K A L Y O N D U G B

64

W O B Y Q C O A

1. GRANDPARENTS
2. FEAR
3. CAT FOOD
4. FAMILY
5. LAUGH
6. CRIME
7. UNKNOWN
8. LOVE
9. DOORBELL
10. COOKIE MONSTER
11. COCKTAIL PARTY
12. HOUSEWIFE
13. PIGGYBANK
14. CARWASH
15. HORSESHOE
16. BOMBSHELL
17. PIZZA HUT
18. HAMMERTIME
19. FINDING NEMO
20. PLANECRASH
21. SEVEN UP
22. FISH AND CHIPS
23. NOSEBLEED
24. QUEEN OF HEARTS
25. THUNDERSTORM
26. BABY BOTTLE
27. CANDY CRUSH
28. CHRISTMAS
29. CATWOMAN
30. PARTY ANIMAL
31. FAMILY PHOTO
32. EARLY BIRD
33. LUCKY STAR
34. LOVESONG
35. MILK CHOCOLATE
36. HARRY POTTER
37. SCARY MOVIE
38. HORSEPOWER
39. DOG FOOD
40. BATHROOM
41. TENNIS SHOES
42. SHRIMP COCKTAIL
43. FORTUNE COOKIES
44. LIGHTHOUSE
45. SHOOTING STAR
46. CATFISH
47. ROCKET SCIENCE
48. HAPPY FEET
49. SUNGLASSES
50. MOONWALK
51. PAPERCUT
52. LOVE STORY
53. ITUNES
54. FIRE ALARM
55. SPIDERMAN
56. BUTCHER
57. MILKSHAKE
58. IPHONE
59. LOVE LETTER
60. WATCHDOG
61. STARFISH
62. BURGER KING
63. LADYBUG
64. COWBOY

EMOJI DRAWING

Learn to draw emojis by following the steps shown below.

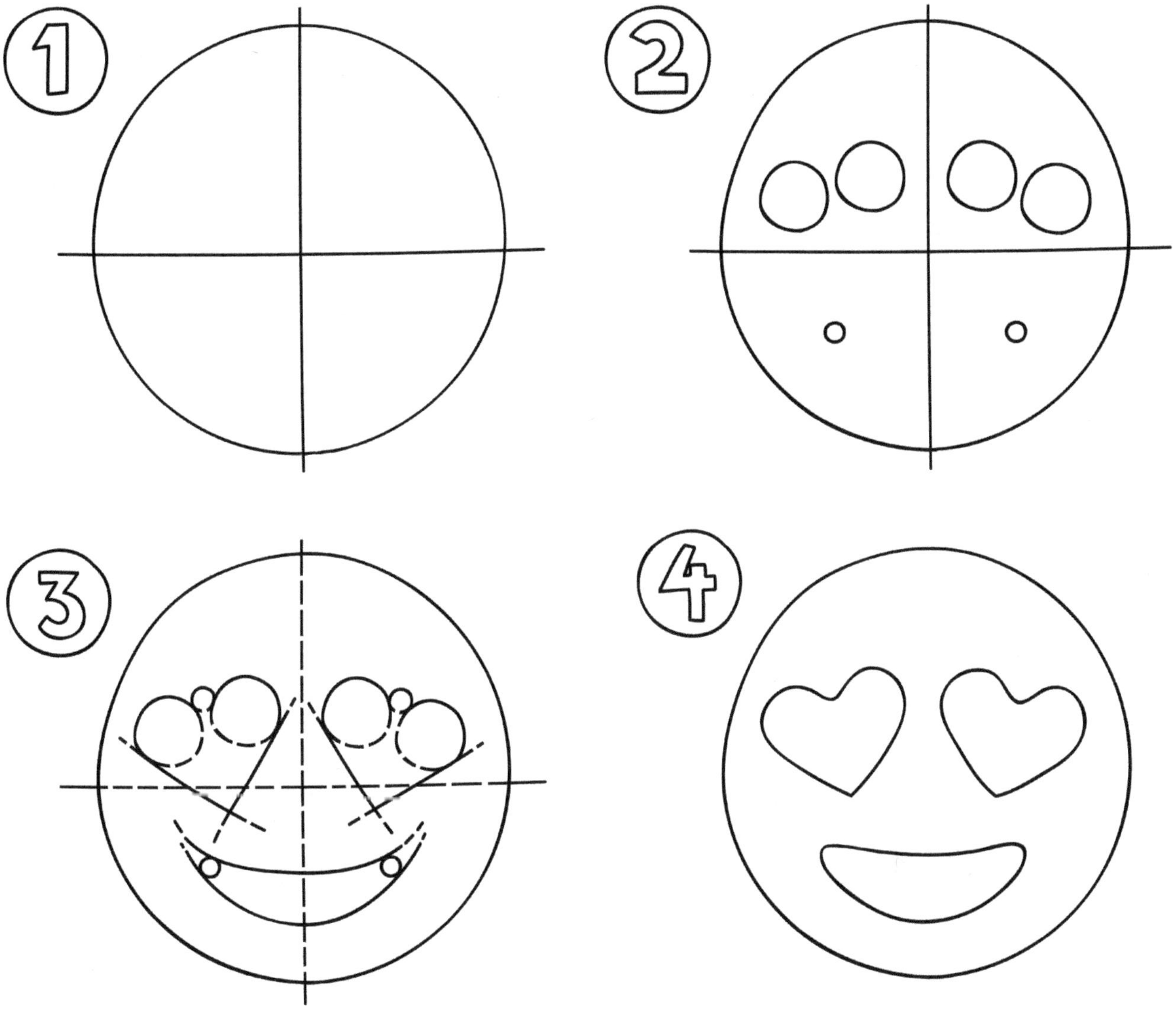
1
2
3
4

YOU TRY

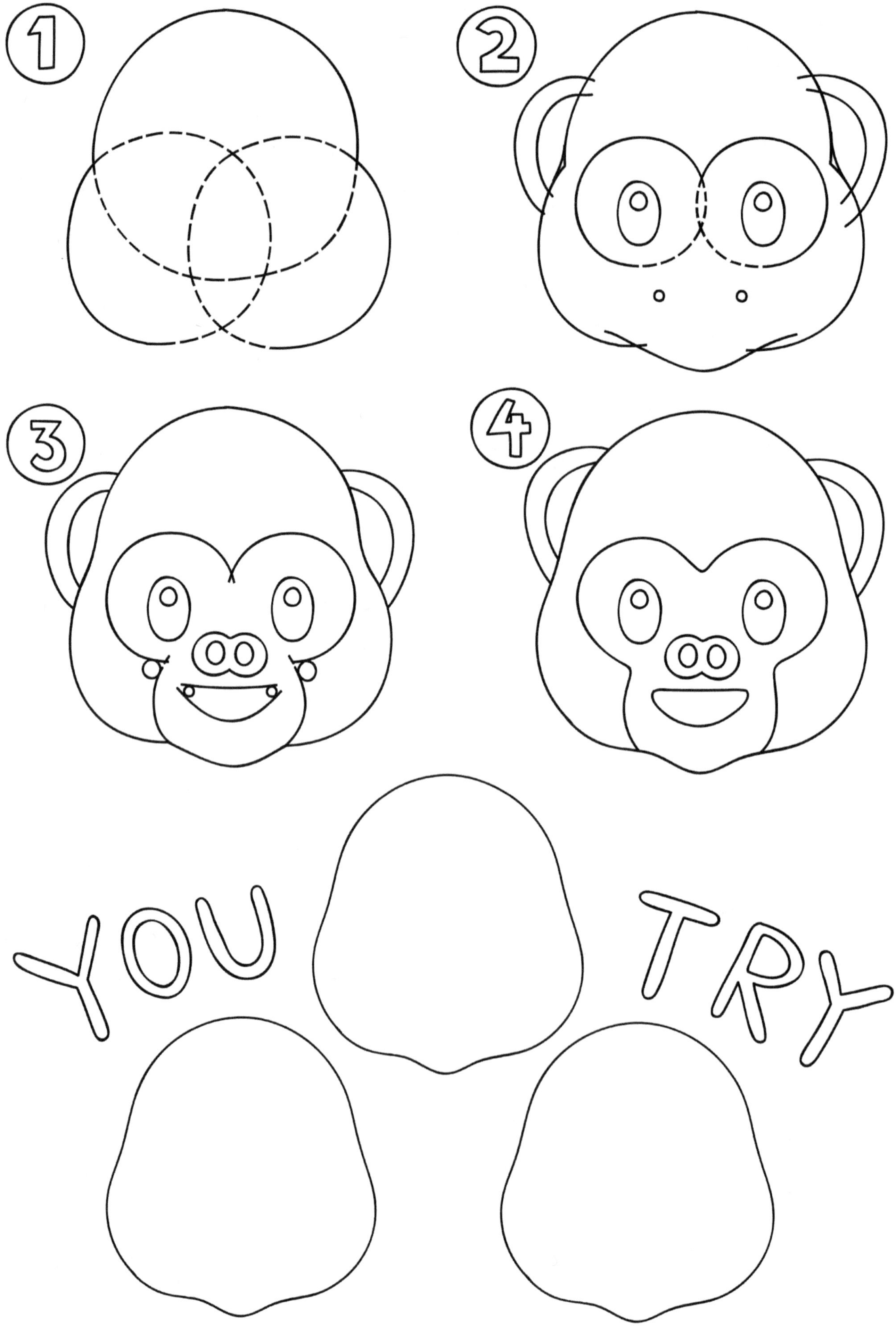
1
2
3
4
YOU TRY

1
2
3
4

YOU TRY

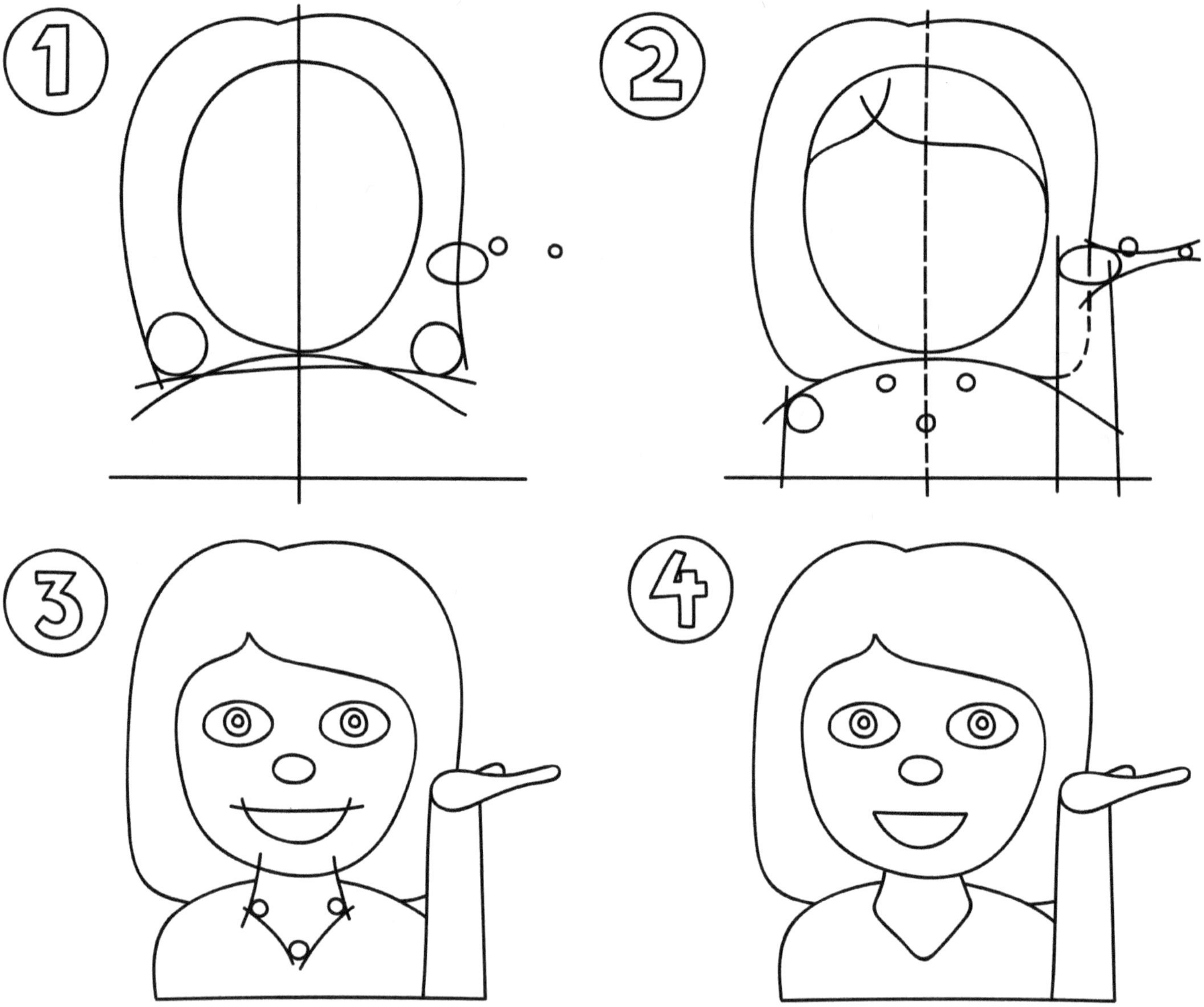

YOU TRY

1
2
3
4
YOU TRY

1

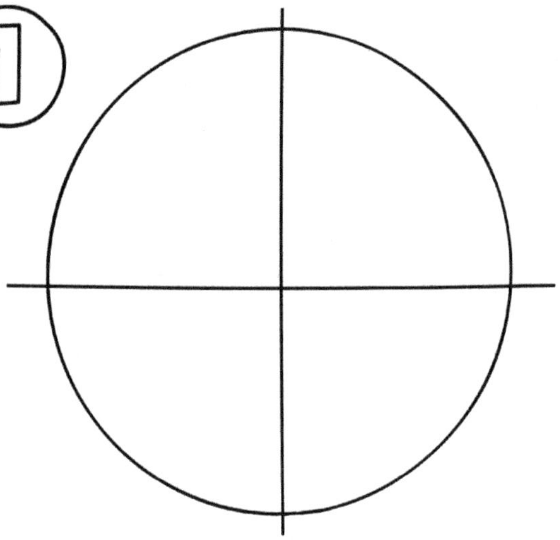

2

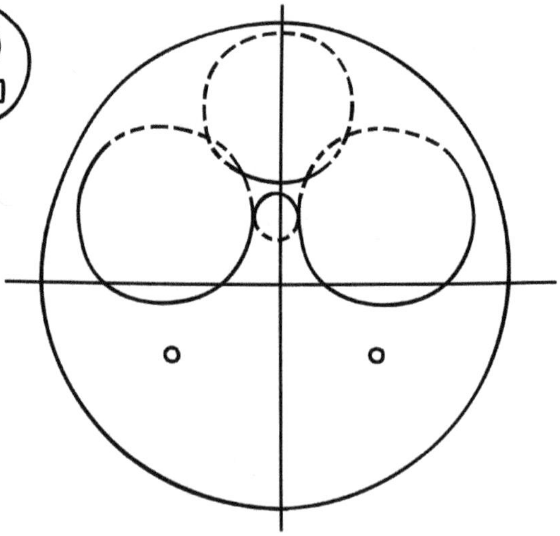

3

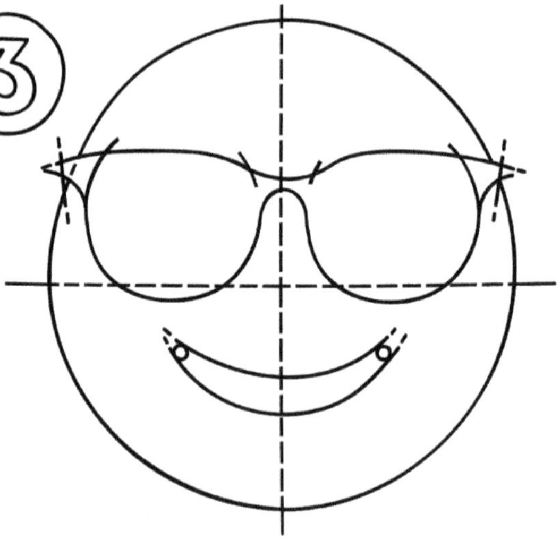

4

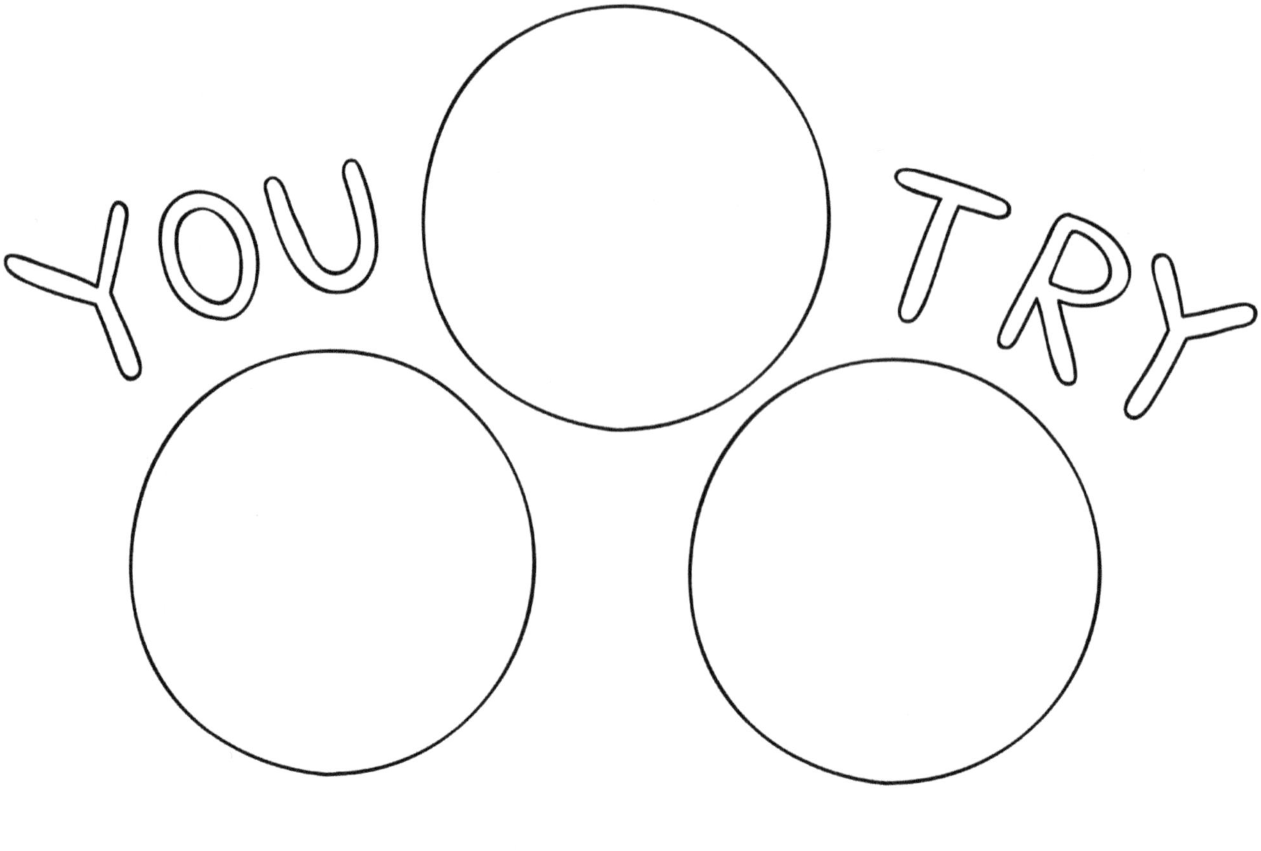

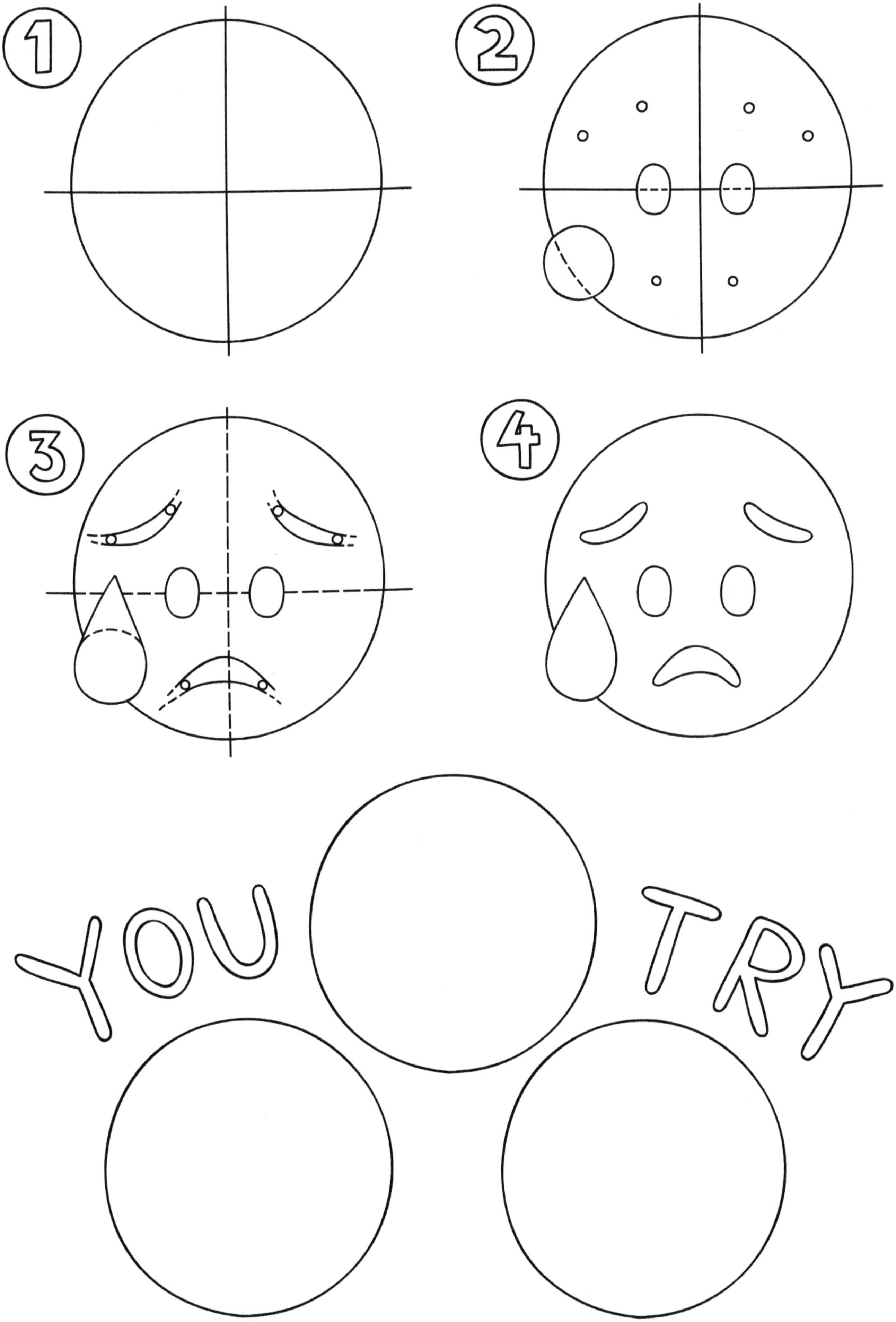
1
2
3
4
YOU TRY

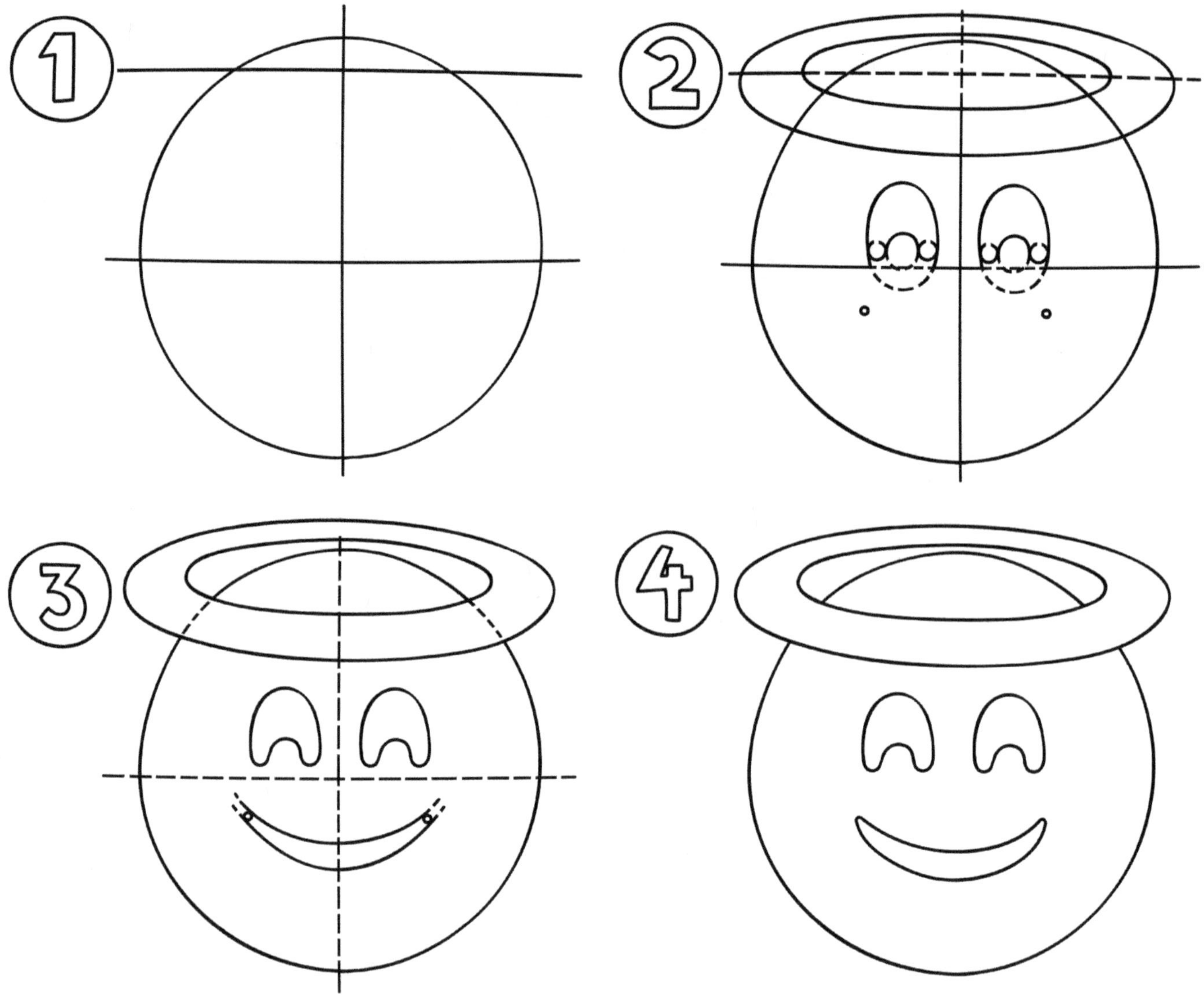
1
2
3
4

YOU TRY

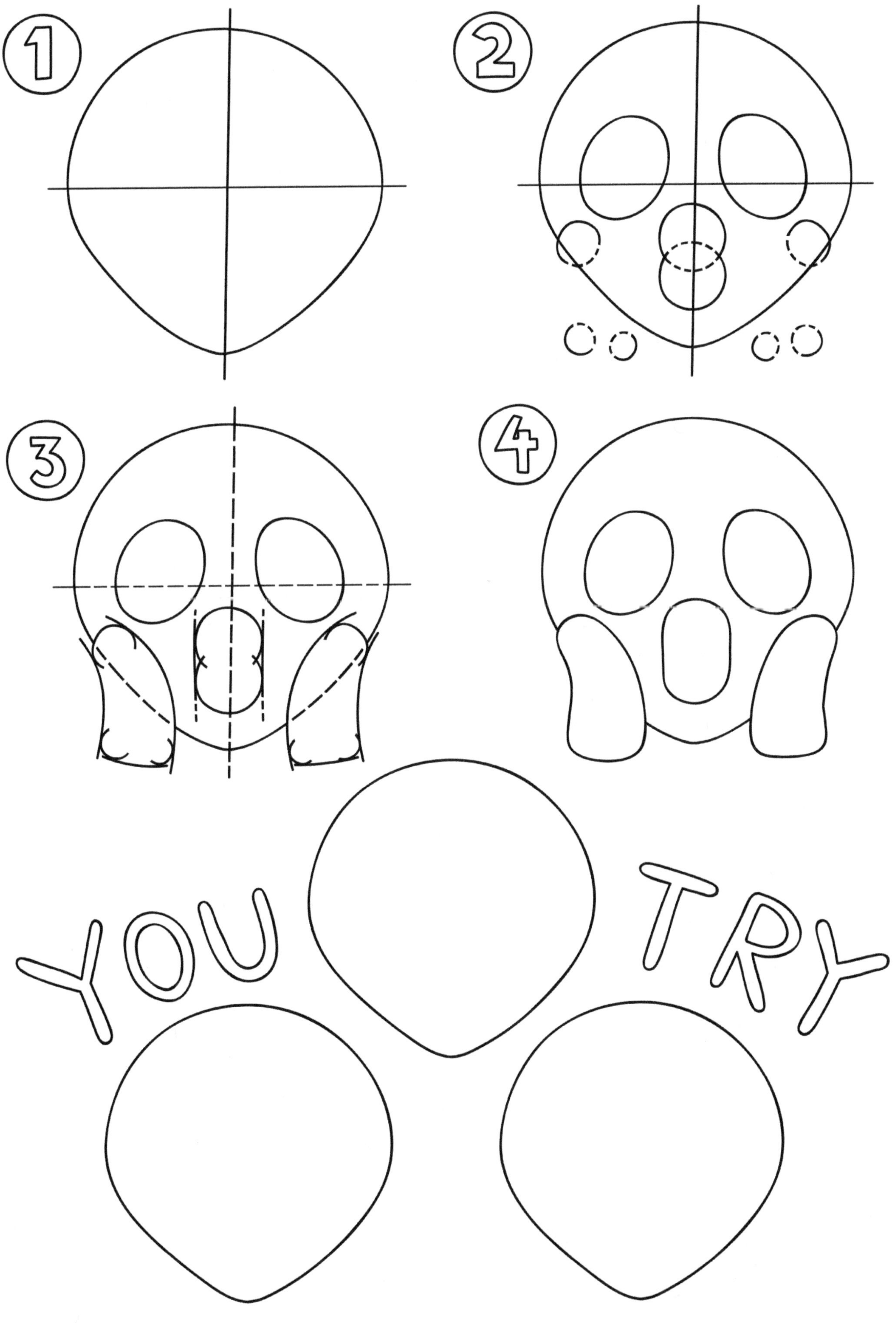
1
2
3
4
YOU TRY

1
2
3
4
YOU
TRY

1

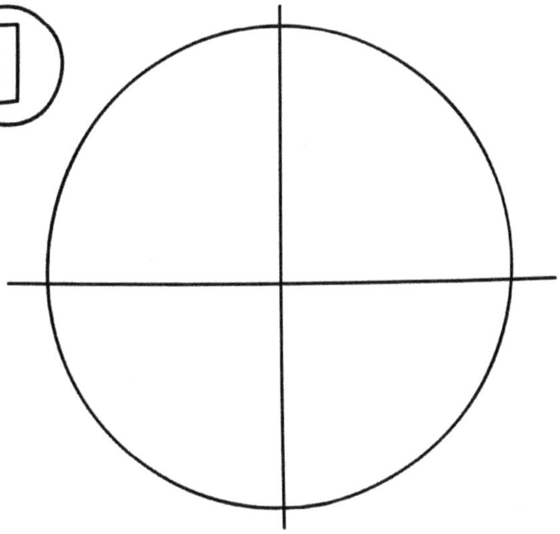

2

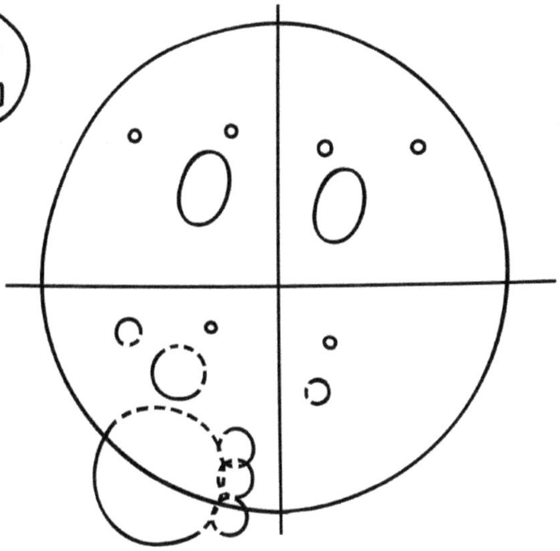

3

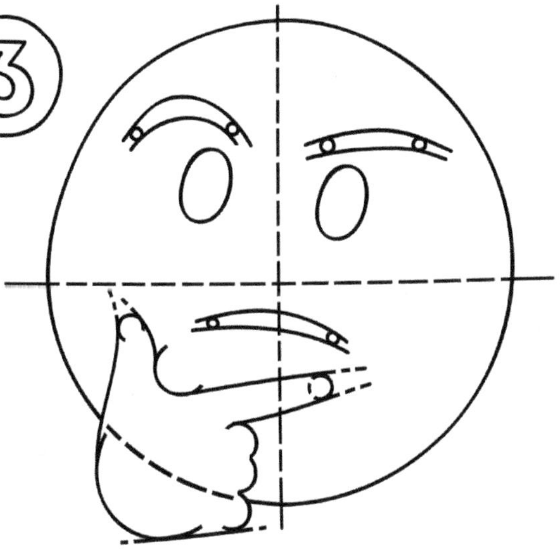

4

YOU TRY

1
2
3
4

YOU DRAW

1
2
3
4
YOU TRY

EMOJI CUT OUTS

1. Color these emoji cut-outs.
2. Cut them out.
3. Fold and glue them together so that they can stand up.

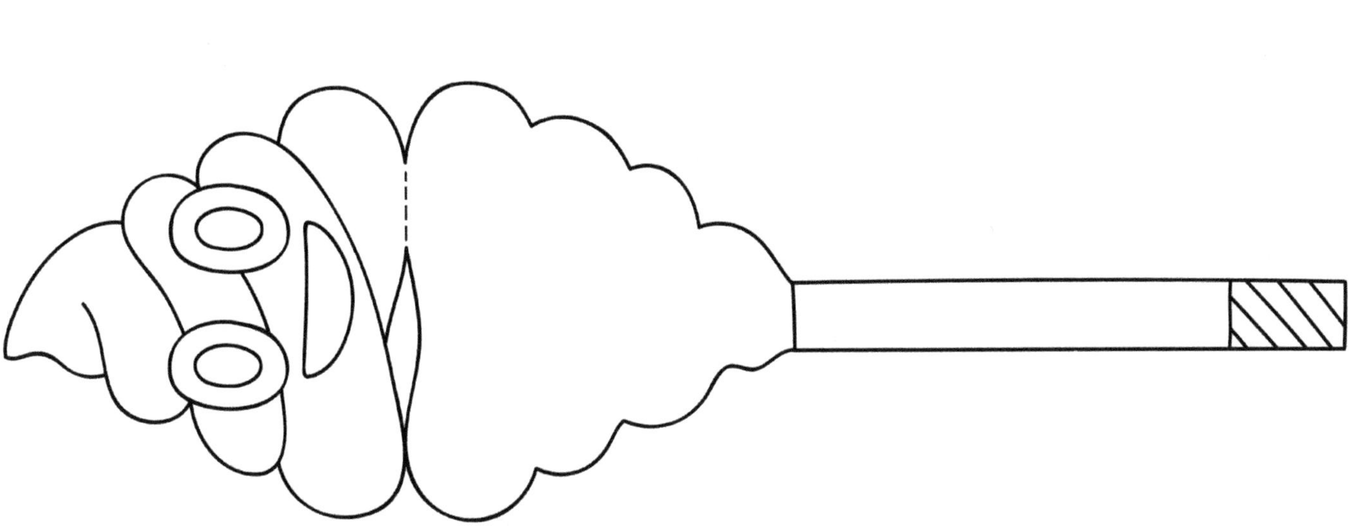

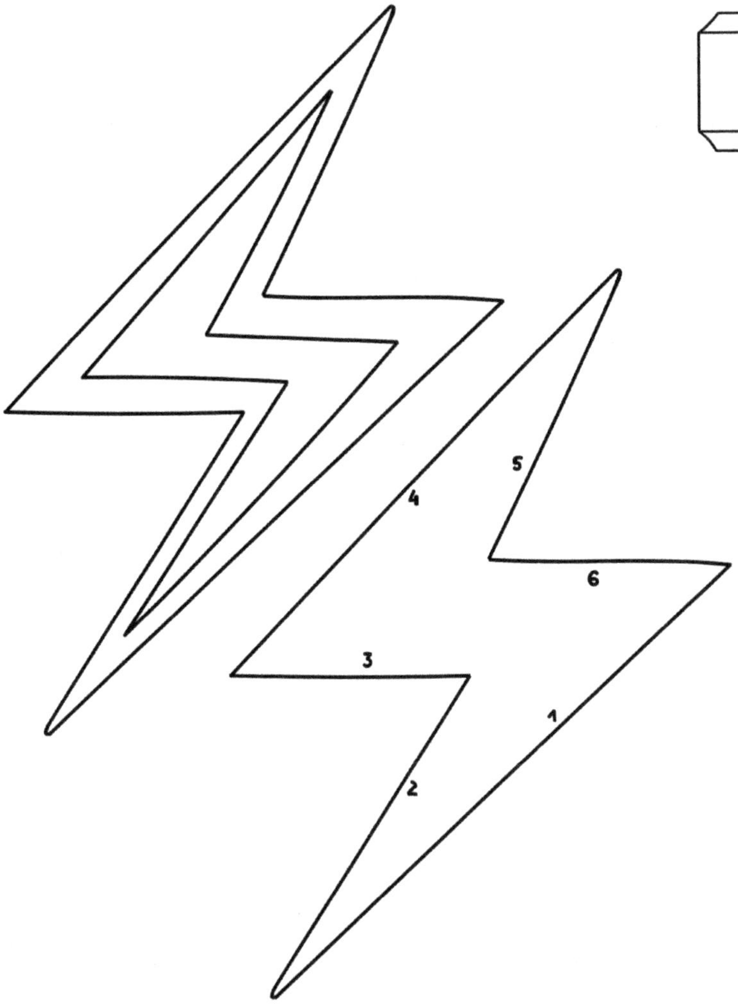

1
2
3
4
5
6

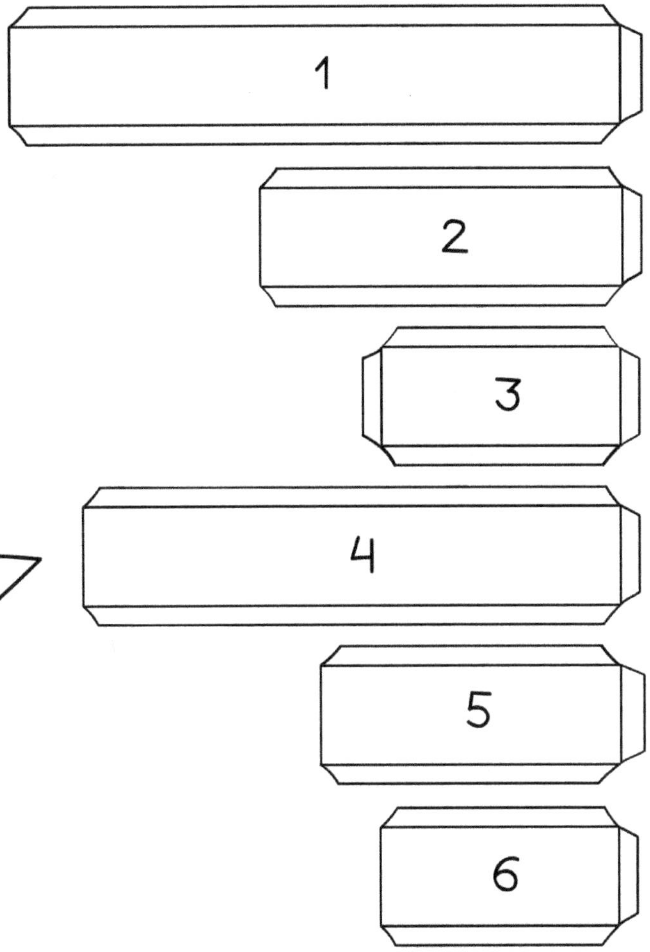

1
2
3
4
5
6

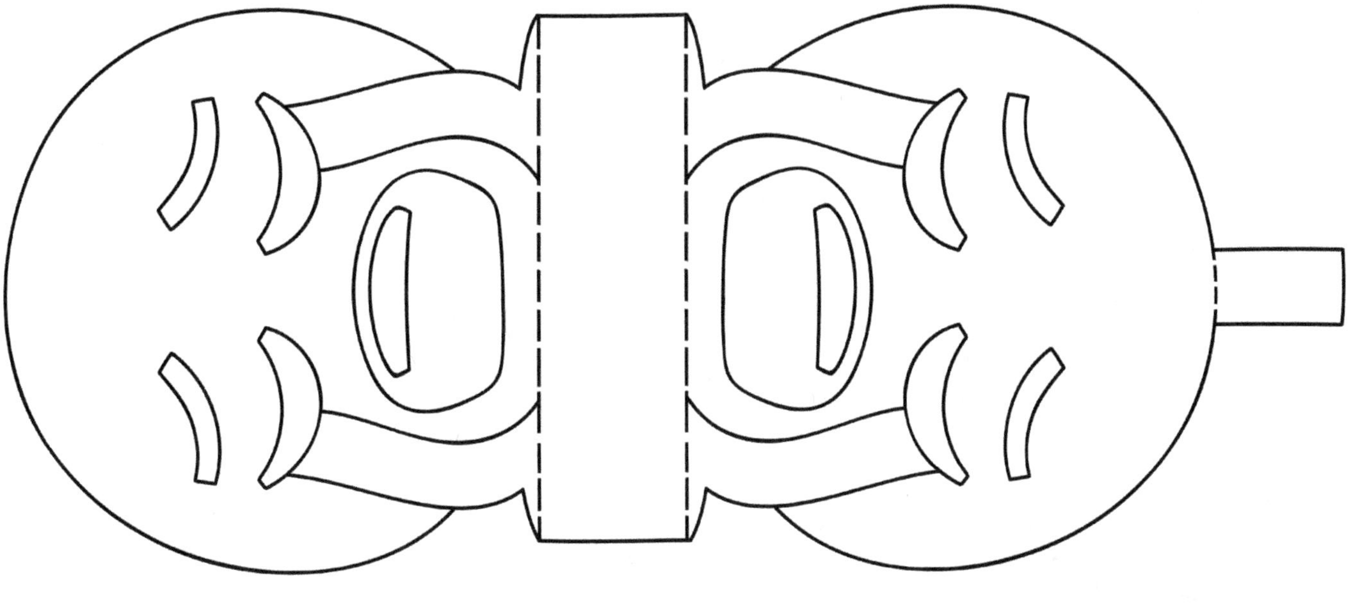

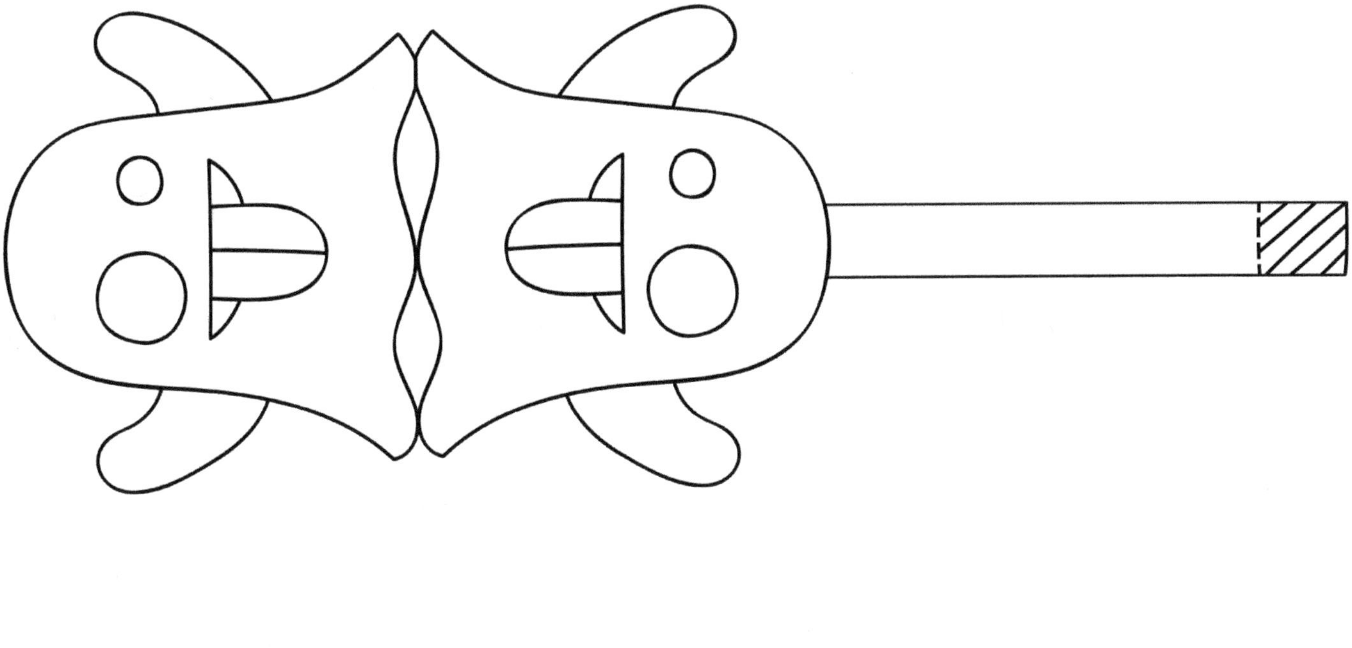

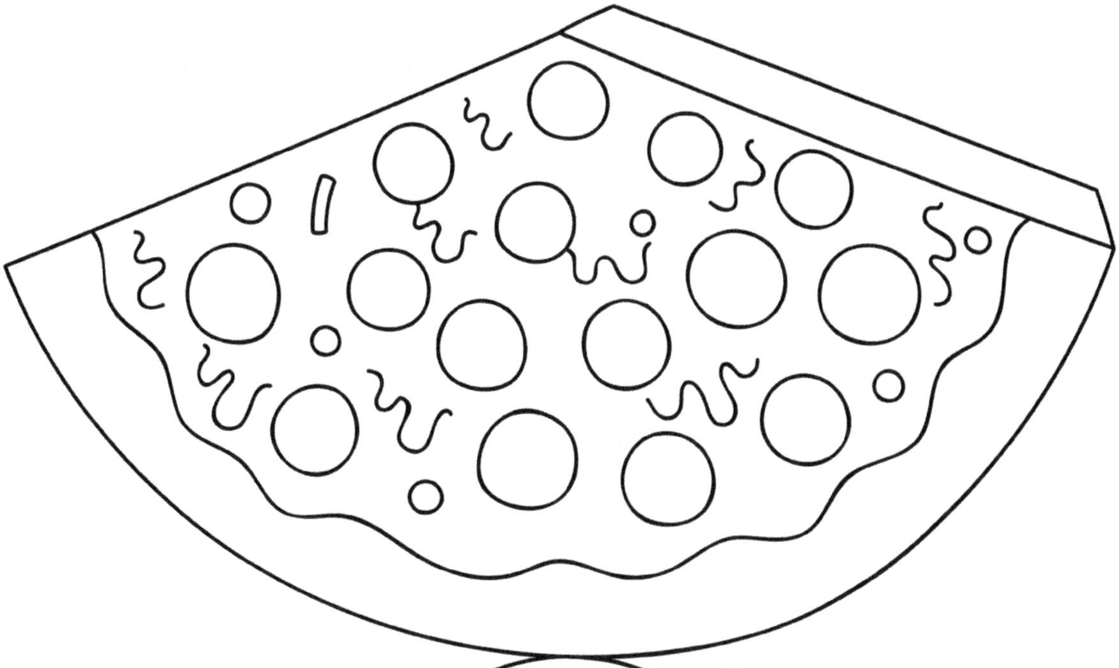

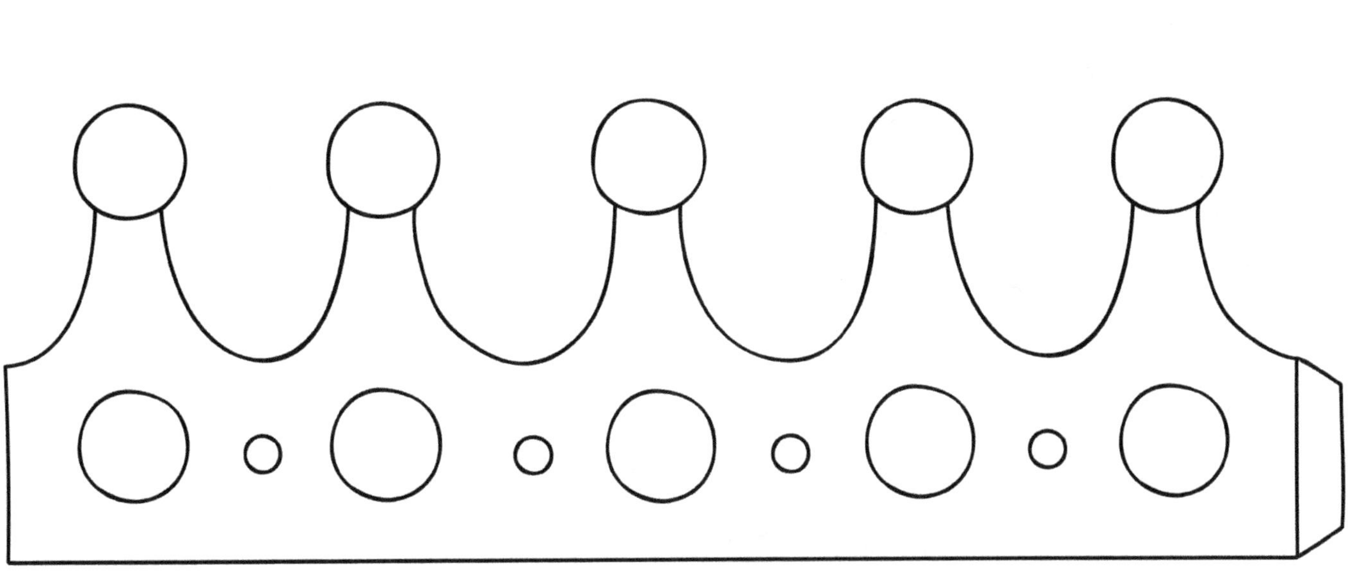

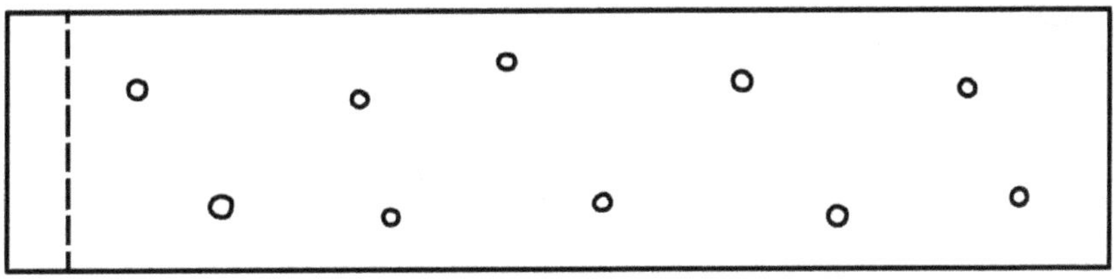

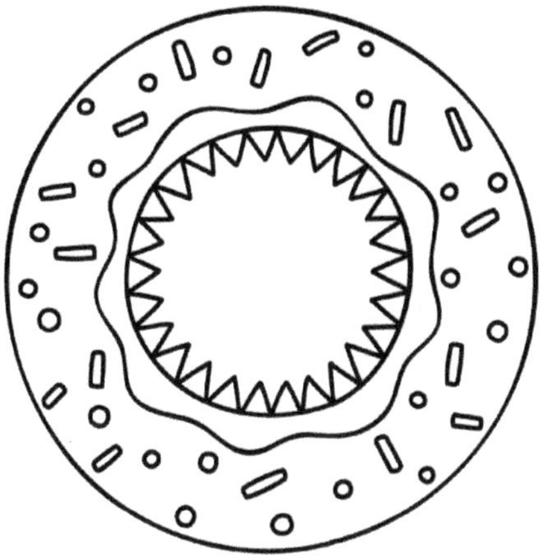

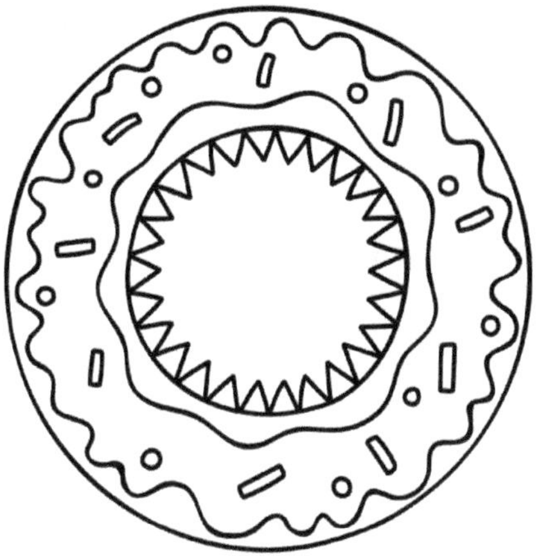

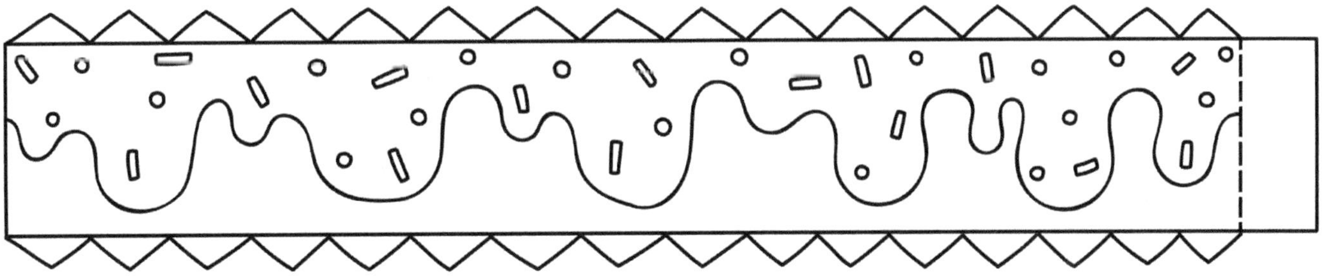

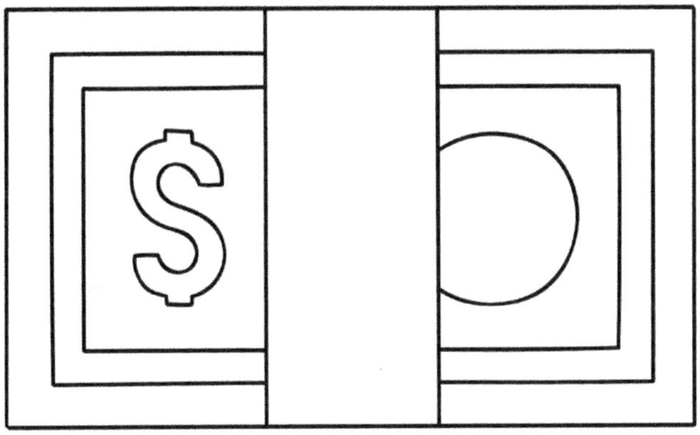
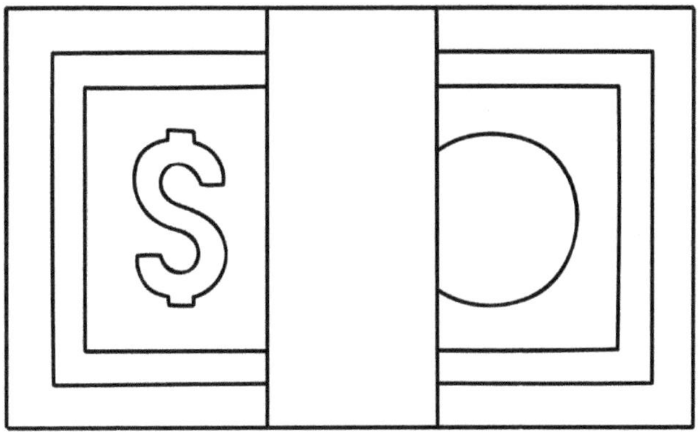
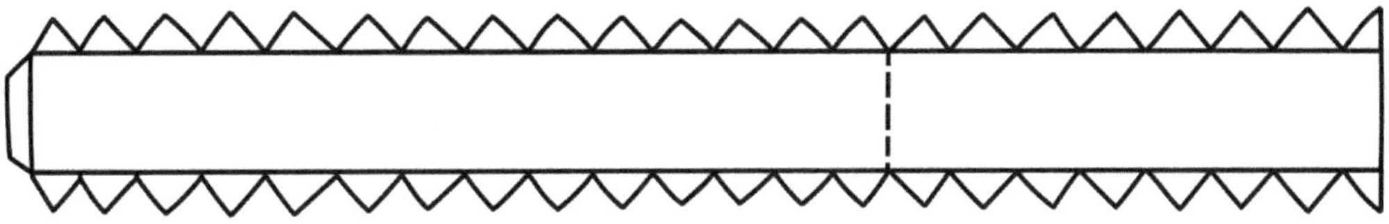
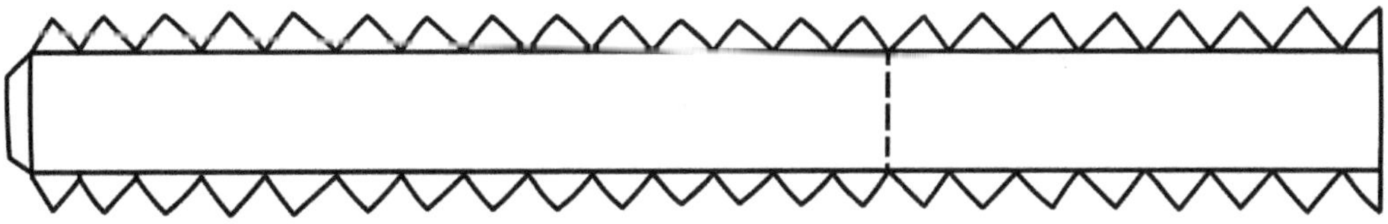
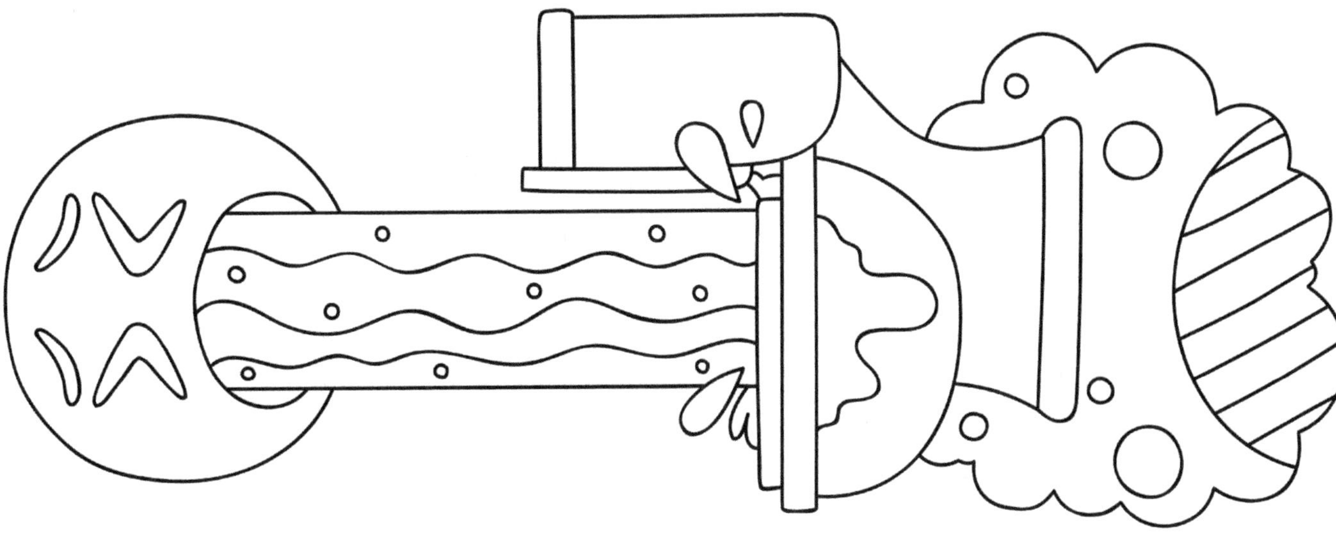

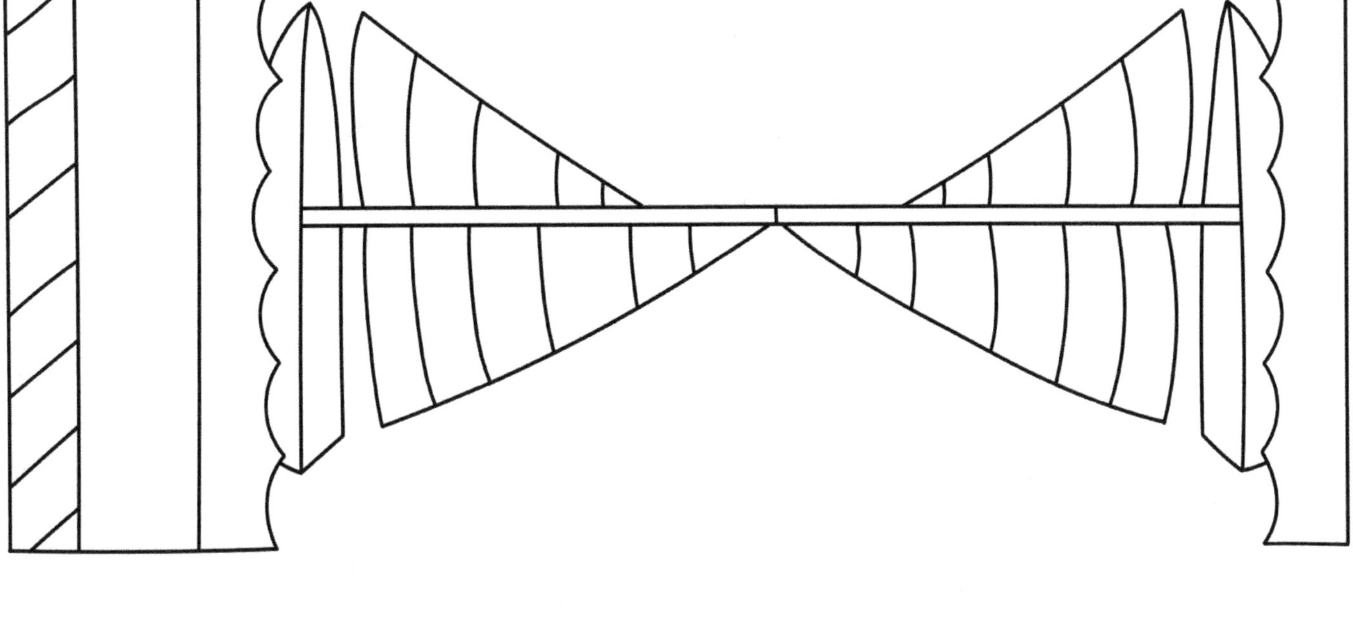

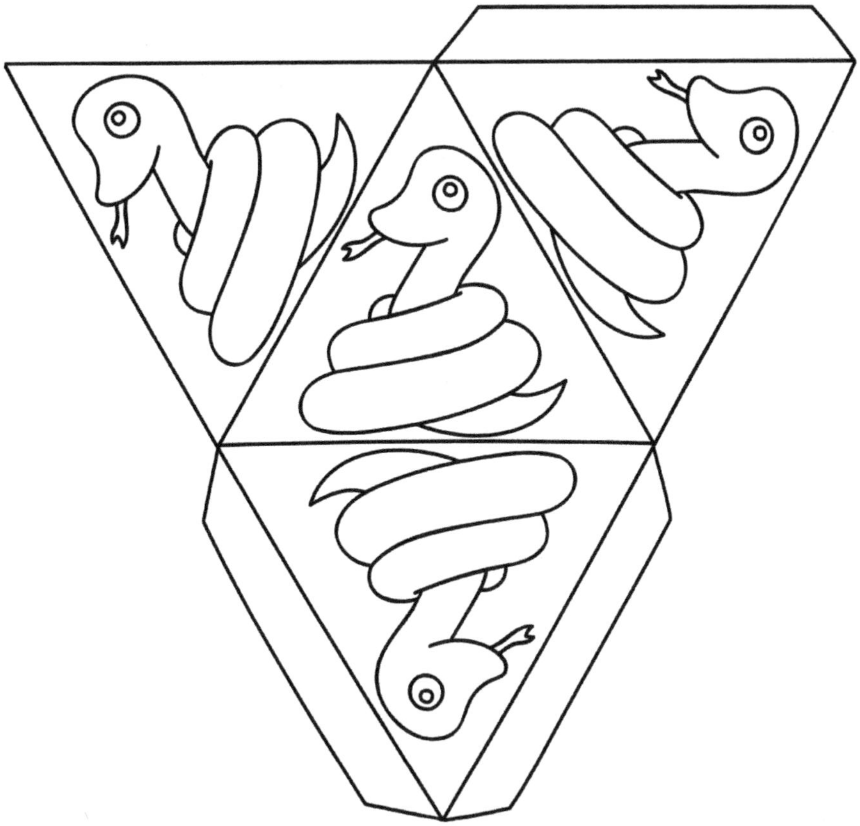

One last thing - we would love to hear your feedback about this book!

If you found this activity book fun and useful, we would be very grateful if you posted a short review on Amazon! Your support does make a difference and we read every review personally.

If you would like to leave a review, just head on over to this book's Amazon page and click "Write a customer review".

Thank you for your support!

www.ingramcontent.com/pod-product-compliance
Lightning Source LLC
LaVergne TN
LVHW082034050326
832904LV00006B/279